JavaScript Web Development Master the Language for Interactive Websites

A Complete Guide to Building Dynamic Websites with JavaScript

MIGUEL FARMER

RAFAEL SANDERS

Table of Content

TABLE OF CONTENTS

INTRODUCTION

Welcome to **"JavaScript Web Development: Master the Language for Interactive Websites"** – a comprehensive guide designed to take you on a journey through the dynamic and exciting world of web development with JavaScript. Whether you're a beginner just starting out or an experienced developer looking to deepen your knowledge, this book provides a clear, hands-on, and structured approach to mastering JavaScript for building modern, interactive, and scalable web applications.

Why JavaScript?

JavaScript is the backbone of modern web development. It is the only programming language that runs natively in all web browsers, enabling you to create interactive, dynamic websites that users love to engage with. From adding interactivity like form validation and animation to building complex, real-time web applications, JavaScript has become an indispensable tool for developers worldwide.

The power of JavaScript lies not just in its ability to run on the front-end, but also its ability to power the back-end with technologies like **Node.js**, allowing developers to build full-stack web applications entirely in JavaScript. Additionally, with the rise of frameworks like **React.js**, **Angular**, and **Vue.js**, JavaScript has evolved from a simple scripting language to a full-fledged ecosystem capable of powering everything from single-page applications to real-time data-driven web apps.

What This Book Covers

In this book, we will dive deep into **JavaScript** and its ecosystem, starting with the basics and gradually progressing to more advanced concepts. Here's a breakdown of the key topics covered:

1. **JavaScript Fundamentals**: We begin by building a solid foundation in JavaScript. This includes understanding its syntax, data structures (like arrays and objects), control structures (like loops and conditionals), and functions. You'll also learn how JavaScript interacts with the web browser, setting the stage for creating interactive and dynamic websites.

2. **Advanced JavaScript Concepts**: Once you're comfortable with the basics, we dive into more advanced JavaScript topics, such as **asynchronous programming**, **closures**, **higher-order functions**, and **ES6+ features** like arrow functions and async/await. These concepts are essential for writing efficient and scalable JavaScript code.

3. **The Document Object Model (DOM)**: JavaScript allows you to interact with the content of your webpage

dynamically. In this section, we'll learn how to manipulate the **DOM** (the structure that represents the content of a webpage), handle user interactions, and update the content in real time.

4. **Building Dynamic Web Applications**: A large part of modern web development involves creating interactive web pages that update based on user input. This section focuses on building interactive web applications using JavaScript, from handling forms and validating inputs to using APIs for dynamic content fetching. We will also explore advanced techniques like **local storage**, **session storage**, and **real-time communication with WebSockets**.

5. **JavaScript Frameworks**: No modern web application is complete without a framework or library. In this book, we cover the basics of **React.js**, one of the most popular JavaScript libraries for building user interfaces. You will learn how to create reusable components, manage application state, and build dynamic interfaces that respond to user interactions.

6. **Backend with JavaScript**: JavaScript isn't just for the front-end. With **Node.js** and **Express**, we'll explore how to build a full-stack web application. You will learn how to set up a server, handle HTTP requests, interact with databases, and deploy your application to production.

7. **Real-World Projects**: We believe in learning by doing. Throughout the book, you'll find hands-on examples and projects that allow you to apply what you've learned. From building simple **to-do apps** to creating full-stack web applications, you'll gain practical experience that will help you build your own projects.

Who This Book Is For

This book is written for anyone who wants to become proficient in JavaScript and web development. Whether you're:

- **A complete beginner**: You'll start with the basics and build your understanding step by step.
- **An intermediate developer**: If you're already familiar with the fundamentals but want to deepen your knowledge and learn best practices, you'll find plenty of advanced topics here.
- **An experienced developer**: Even if you're already a seasoned JavaScript developer, this book provides insights into modern tools, frameworks, and libraries that are essential for full-stack development.

By the end of this book, you'll have a thorough understanding of JavaScript and be able to use it to build both client-side and server-side applications, from static websites to dynamic, interactive web apps.

Why This Book?

JavaScript is one of the most widely-used languages in web development, and its ecosystem is constantly evolving. But with so many libraries, tools, and concepts to learn, it can feel overwhelming. That's where this book comes in. Here's why it stands out:

- **Comprehensive Coverage**: This book offers a structured, step-by-step approach that ensures you gain a deep understanding of JavaScript.
- **Hands-on Examples**: With real-world projects and examples, you'll not only learn the theory but also how to apply it in practical situations.
- **Clear Explanations**: We break down complex concepts into easy-to-understand explanations, making it accessible to both beginners and experienced developers.
- **Up-to-date Practices**: We focus on modern JavaScript features, frameworks, and best practices, ensuring that the skills you learn are relevant to today's web development industry.

How to Use This Book

This book is designed to be read sequentially, as the concepts build on one another. You'll start with the fundamentals and progress through more advanced topics. Each chapter contains hands-on examples that demonstrate how to use JavaScript in real-world scenarios, followed by exercises and projects that help reinforce what you've learned.

- **Beginner-Level Developers**: If you are new to JavaScript, work through each chapter in order and complete the exercises. This will build your skills step by step.
- **Intermediate/Advanced Developers**: If you're already familiar with basic JavaScript, you can focus on specific chapters related to advanced concepts, frameworks, or full-stack development.
- **Practice Makes Perfect**: Don't just read through the code – write your own, experiment with modifications, and build your projects. The more you practice, the more you'll internalize the concepts.

What You Will Achieve

By the end of this book, you will:

- Master **JavaScript syntax**, including advanced features like closures, promises, and asynchronous programming.
- Build interactive websites using **JavaScript** and the **DOM**.
- Develop real-world applications using **React.js** and **Node.js**.
- Understand **full-stack development** with JavaScript and build web applications that connect the front-end with the back-end using **Express** and **MongoDB**.
- Gain a deep understanding of **modern web security**, testing, and debugging techniques, ensuring that your applications are both functional and secure.
- Be able to **deploy** your web applications and make them accessible to users worldwide.

Conclusion

JavaScript is an essential tool for modern web development, and this book is designed to make you a proficient JavaScript developer, whether you are building simple interactive websites or full-stack web applications. With detailed explanations, real-world examples, and hands-on projects, you will gain the skills necessary to bring your ideas to life on the web.

Let's begin your journey into the world of JavaScript web development, where you'll master the language, create dynamic websites, and build powerful, interactive web applications.

Part 1

Introduction to JavaScript and Web Development Fundamentals

CHAPTER 1

INTRODUCTION TO WEB DEVELOPMENT

Overview of Web Development

Web development refers to the creation and maintenance of websites and web applications. It encompasses everything that goes into building a website from the ground up, including design, functionality, content management, and interactivity. Whether you're creating a simple static website or a dynamic web application, web development is an essential skill for anyone looking to build an online presence.

In the early days of the web, websites were static, meaning their content did not change unless manually updated. However, over time, the web has evolved to allow for more interactive, dynamic, and responsive websites that provide a rich user experience. Modern web development uses a combination of technologies and programming languages to deliver complex features, making it possible to develop everything from blogs to social networks to online stores.

Front-End vs. Back-End

Web development is typically divided into two main areas: **front-end** and **back-end**. Understanding the difference between these two is crucial for anyone looking to get into web development.

1. **Front-End Development**
   o **What It Is**: The front-end is everything that users interact with directly in their web browsers. It's what people see and engage with when they visit a website. This includes the layout, design, structure, and any interactive elements of a webpage.
   o **Technologies Used**:
      ▪ **HTML** (Hypertext Markup Language) defines the structure of a webpage.
      ▪ **CSS** (Cascading Style Sheets) controls the presentation, including colors, fonts, and layouts.
      ▪ **JavaScript** adds interactivity to a webpage by allowing you to manipulate HTML and CSS dynamically.
   o **Key Role**: A front-end developer focuses on creating an intuitive, user-friendly experience by optimizing the appearance and interactivity of a website. They ensure that users can easily navigate the site and engage with its content.

2. **Back-End Development**

- o **What It Is**: The back-end is the server side of a website. It involves managing the data, logic, and the overall structure of a website that users don't see. Back-end development involves creating the code that handles the communication between the user's browser and the database or server that stores and processes information.

- o **Technologies Used**:
  - **Server-side languages** like Python, Ruby, PHP, Java, and JavaScript (with Node.js).
  - **Databases** like MySQL, MongoDB, and PostgreSQL.
  - **Server** technologies, such as Apache or Nginx.

- o **Key Role**: A back-end developer is responsible for managing the database, handling user authentication, and ensuring the site functions correctly behind the scenes. They make sure that the front-end has the data it needs to display to users and that any interactions are processed smoothly.

Introduction to JavaScript: The Language of the Web

JavaScript is one of the core technologies of web development, alongside HTML and CSS. While HTML provides the structure and CSS handles the styling, JavaScript is the language that makes websites interactive. It allows developers to manipulate the content and behavior of a webpage dynamically, creating a more engaging and interactive experience for users.

JavaScript is a **client-side scripting language**, meaning it runs directly in the user's browser rather than on a web server. This gives developers the ability to create fast, real-time interactions without needing to constantly reload the page or make requests to the server. JavaScript's versatility has made it the most popular programming language for web development, powering everything from form validations to complex animations and interactive maps.

Why JavaScript?

- **Universality**: It runs on all major browsers (Chrome, Firefox, Safari, Edge), so you don't need to worry about compatibility issues.
- **Event-driven**: JavaScript responds to events like clicks, mouse movements, and keyboard inputs, allowing for real-time interaction.

- **Asynchronous**: JavaScript allows you to perform tasks (like loading data) in the background without interrupting the user experience.

- **Growing Ecosystem**: There's a vast library of frameworks and tools built on top of JavaScript, such as React, Vue, and Angular, that allow you to build complex applications with ease.

Real-World Example: The Evolution of Modern Websites

The evolution of modern websites is a fascinating journey that highlights the power and capabilities of JavaScript in shaping the user experience.

1. **Early   Websites**:
   In the early days of the web, websites were simple and static. They consisted of HTML pages with basic text and images. There was no interactivity beyond clicking links to navigate to new pages. These websites were primarily informational, with little to no dynamic content. Think of early search engines like Yahoo! or simple blogs.

2. **Web   2.0   (Dynamic   Content)**:
   With the rise of Web 2.0 in the early 2000s, websites became more interactive. JavaScript played a pivotal role by enabling dynamic content changes without requiring the page to reload. For example, Gmail and Facebook

introduced features like live updates, chat systems, and user interaction that didn't require a page refresh. These sites utilized JavaScript to handle asynchronous requests (AJAX) and manipulate the DOM (Document Object Model) in real-time.

3. **Responsive and Mobile-Friendly Websites**: As smartphones and tablets became more popular, websites had to adapt to different screen sizes. JavaScript frameworks and libraries, such as Bootstrap and jQuery, made it easier to create responsive websites that adjusted to various screen sizes and devices. JavaScript also played a role in touch events and gestures, such as swiping and pinch-to-zoom, improving the mobile experience.

4. **Single-Page Applications (SPAs)**: Modern websites often load content dynamically within a single page, rather than requiring the browser to reload an entirely new page each time a user clicks a link. SPAs like Google Maps, Instagram, and Twitter rely heavily on JavaScript to provide seamless navigation and update content in real-time, making the user experience feel instantaneous.

5. **Interactive Front-End Frameworks**: More recently, JavaScript frameworks like **React**, **Vue.js**, and **Angular** have revolutionized how we build interactive websites and web applications. These frameworks allow developers to create sophisticated user

interfaces and manage state efficiently, making JavaScript more powerful than ever.

Takeaway: The evolution of modern websites—from simple HTML pages to fully dynamic, interactive, and mobile-friendly applications—illustrates the incredible journey of JavaScript and its central role in shaping the web. As JavaScript continues to evolve, it remains the backbone of modern web development, enabling developers to create powerful, interactive websites that users engage with every day.

This chapter gives a foundational understanding of web development and introduces JavaScript as the key language driving interactivity and dynamic content on the web. The real-world example showcases how JavaScript has evolved alongside modern web development trends, setting the stage for the deeper dive into JavaScript in the chapters to follow.

CHAPTER 2

SETTING UP YOUR DEVELOPMENT ENVIRONMENT

Installing Node.js, npm, and VS Code

To start developing in JavaScript and become an effective web developer, it's essential to set up a development environment. This chapter will guide you through installing the necessary tools that will enable you to write, test, and run JavaScript code on your local machine.

1. **Installing**   **Node.js**

   Node.js is a runtime environment that allows you to run JavaScript on the server side, outside the browser. It's built on Google Chrome's V8 JavaScript engine and is widely used for backend development, as well as for managing tools and packages with npm (Node Package Manager).

   Steps to Install Node.js:

   o Visit the official Node.js website: https://nodejs.org/

23

- o Choose the version recommended for most users (LTS version) and download it for your operating system (Windows, macOS, or Linux).
- o Once downloaded, run the installer and follow the on-screen instructions.
- o After installation, confirm that Node.js is installed by opening a terminal (or command prompt) and typing the following command:

```bash
node -v
```

This will display the version of Node.js installed on your system.

2. **Installing npm (Node Package Manager)** npm comes bundled with Node.js and allows you to easily manage libraries and dependencies for your JavaScript projects. It simplifies the process of installing, updating, and managing third-party libraries or packages.

To check if npm is installed, open a terminal or command prompt and type:

```bash
npm -v
```

This will show the installed version of npm. If it's correctly installed, you're all set to use npm in your projects.

3. **Installing Visual Studio Code (VS Code)**
Visual Studio Code (VS Code) is a lightweight yet powerful source code editor used by developers to write JavaScript and other languages. It comes with essential features like syntax highlighting, IntelliSense (auto-completion of code), debugging support, and an integrated terminal.

Steps to Install VS Code:

- o Go to the official website: https://code.visualstudio.com/
- o Download the installer for your operating system.
- o Follow the installation instructions and launch the application once it's installed.

Setting Up VS Code for JavaScript:

- o Once VS Code is installed, open the editor and navigate to the Extensions tab (on the left sidebar).
- o Search for **"JavaScript (ES6) code snippets"** and **"Prettier"** to install the popular extensions

that provide enhanced JavaScript support and auto-formatting.

o Now, you're ready to write JavaScript code in a professional environment.

Introduction to Web Browsers and Developer Tools

Web browsers are the primary tools through which users access websites. As a developer, you will use browsers to test and debug your JavaScript code.

1. **Web** **Browsers**

There are several web browsers available for testing and running your code. The most common ones include:

o **Google Chrome**

o **Mozilla Firefox**

o **Safari** (macOS only)

o **Microsoft Edge**

Why **Google** **Chrome?**

For web development, Google Chrome is widely preferred due to its robust **Developer Tools** (DevTools), which allow you to inspect HTML, CSS, and JavaScript in real-time.

2. **Developer Tools in Web Browsers**

All modern browsers come with built-in developer tools, but for this guide, we'll focus on Chrome's DevTools.

Accessing Chrome DevTools:

○ Open Chrome, and navigate to a website.

○ Right-click anywhere on the page and click **Inspect** (or press `Ctrl + Shift + I` on Windows/Linux, or `Cmd + Option + I` on macOS).

Key Features of DevTools:

○ **Elements Panel**: View and edit the HTML structure of the page.

○ **Console Panel**: View messages, errors, and logs generated by JavaScript.

○ **Network Panel**: Track network activity, including HTTP requests and responses.

○ **Sources Panel**: Debug JavaScript code with breakpoints and step-through execution.

Real-time   Debugging:

You can use the **Console** to test small snippets of JavaScript. For example, if you want to test if your `console.log()` statement works, open the Console and type:

```
javascript
```

```
console.log('Hello, world!');
```

Press Enter, and you'll see the output appear in the console. This is an essential tool for testing and troubleshooting JavaScript code.

How to Write Your First JavaScript Code

Now that you have your development environment set up, it's time to write some code. JavaScript is a versatile language that can be used to create interactive and dynamic elements in a webpage.

1. **Creating   Your   First   HTML   File**
   First, let's create a basic HTML file to work with. In VS Code, create a new file and save it as index.html. Inside this file, write the following:

```
html
```

```
<!DOCTYPE html>
<html lang="en">
<head>
    <meta charset="UTF-8">
    <meta                name="viewport"
content="width=device-width,     initial-
scale=1.0">
```

```
<title>My First JavaScript</title>
</head>
<body>
    <h1>Welcome to JavaScript</h1>
    <p id="greeting">Hello, Visitor!</p>

    <script src="app.js"></script>
</body>
</html>
```

2. **Creating Your First JavaScript File**

   Now, let's add some JavaScript code. In the same folder as index.html, create a new file called app.js. Inside this file, write the following:

   javascript

```
// This is a comment. The next line will
change the text content of the paragraph.
document.getElementById('greeting').textC
ontent = 'Hello, JavaScript!';
```

3. **Running Your Code**

   o   Open the index.html file in your web browser (by double-clicking on it).

   o   You should see the page with the text "Hello, Visitor!" change to "Hello, JavaScript!" when the JavaScript code runs.

This simple example demonstrates how JavaScript interacts with the DOM (Document Object Model) to modify the content of a webpage. In this case, we used JavaScript to change the text of a <p> tag.

Real-World Example: Your First "Hello World" Web Page

A classic example of a first JavaScript program is the "Hello World" webpage. This example demonstrates how to create a basic webpage that interacts with the user.

1. **Creating the HTML**: In your index.html file, add a button that, when clicked, will trigger a JavaScript function.

html

```html
<!DOCTYPE html>
<html lang="en">
<head>
    <meta charset="UTF-8">
    <meta                     name="viewport"
content="width=device-width,       initial-
scale=1.0">
    <title>Hello World</title>
</head>
<body>
    <h1>JavaScript Web Development</h1>
```

```
    <button              id="clickMe">Click
Me!</button>
    <p id="message"></p>

    <script src="app.js"></script>
</body>
</html>
```

2. **Adding JavaScript**: In your `app.js` file, write the following code to handle the button click event:

```
javascript

document.getElementById('clickMe').addEve
ntListener('click', function() {

document.getElementById('message').textCo
ntent = 'Hello, World! JavaScript is
awesome!';
});
```

3. **Running the Code**:
   o   Open `index.html` in a browser.
   o   Click the "Click Me!" button.
   o   The text "Hello, World! JavaScript is awesome!" should appear below the button.

This is a simple, interactive "Hello World" web page that demonstrates the basics of JavaScript event handling and

31

DOM manipulation. It's a great starting point for building more complex interactive applications.

Summary

In this chapter, you:

- Installed the necessary tools (Node.js, npm, and VS Code) to start JavaScript development.
- Explored web browsers and their developer tools for debugging and testing JavaScript.
- Wrote your first JavaScript code to interact with a webpage.
- Built a basic interactive "Hello World" example that demonstrated event handling and DOM manipulation.

These foundational steps will serve as the building blocks for more advanced JavaScript concepts and applications as you continue learning web development.

A network error occurred. Please check your connection and try again. If this issue persists please contact us through our help center at help.openai.com.

CHAPTER 3

UNDERSTANDING HTML AND CSS FOR JAVASCRIPT INTEGRATION

The Relationship Between HTML, CSS, and JavaScript

When developing a website or web application, three core technologies work together to bring your project to life: **HTML**, **CSS**, and **JavaScript**. While each technology serves a unique purpose, they are closely intertwined to create an engaging and functional user experience.

1. **HTML (Hypertext Markup Language)**: HTML is the backbone of any web page. It provides the structure and content. Without HTML, there would be no web page to display. It's a markup language used to structure the web content like text, images, links, and forms.

    o **Key Role**: Defines the structure and layout of web pages.

33

o **Tags**: HTML uses tags such as `<div>`, `<h1>`, `<p>`, and `<a>` to mark different elements on the page.

2. **CSS (Cascading Style Sheets)**: While HTML gives structure, **CSS** controls the presentation. It is used to style and position elements, defining how a page looks (e.g., colors, fonts, margins). CSS allows web designers and developers to create visually appealing and consistent web pages.

   o **Key Role**: Handles the visual aspects such as layout, design, and responsiveness.

   o **Selectors and Properties**: CSS uses selectors (e.g., `div`, `.class-name`, `#id-name`) to target HTML elements and apply styles.

3. **JavaScript**:
   JavaScript adds interactivity to web pages. It allows you to modify HTML and CSS dynamically, creating responsive and interactive user experiences. JavaScript can respond to user actions like clicks, typing, or page load events, and alter the content and style of the page without needing to reload it.

   o **Key Role**: Adds interactivity and dynamic content changes.

   o **Integration**: JavaScript can manipulate HTML (DOM) and CSS (styles) in real-time, allowing you to make webpages come alive.

Structuring HTML and Styling with CSS

Before diving into JavaScript, it's important to understand how to structure a webpage using **HTML** and **CSS**, as JavaScript will interact with these elements. Let's walk through the basics.

1. **HTML** **Structure**:

   A basic HTML document follows a simple structure:

   html

```
<!DOCTYPE html>
<html lang="en">
<head>
    <meta charset="UTF-8">
    <meta                name="viewport"
content="width=device-width,      initial-
scale=1.0">
    <title>Interactive Web Page</title>
    <link                 rel="stylesheet"
href="styles.css">
</head>
<body>
    <header>
        <h1>Welcome to My Interactive Web
Page</h1>
    </header>
    <main>
```

```
        <p>This is a simple paragraph with
some <strong>important</strong> text.</p>
        <button    id="changeTextBtn">Click
me</button>
        <div id="contentBox"></div>
    </main>
    <footer>
        <p>© 2025 My Website</p>
    </footer>
    <script src="app.js"></script>
</body>
</html>
```

- o **Explanation**:
  - The <html> element is the root of the webpage.
  - The <head> section contains meta-information, including the title of the page and links to external resources like the CSS file.
  - The <body> section contains the content that is displayed to users, including headings, paragraphs, buttons, and divs.
  - The <script> tag at the bottom includes your JavaScript file.

2. **CSS** **Styling**:

CSS controls how the HTML elements look. You can

style elements using selectors and properties. Here's a basic example of how to style the HTML structure above:

css

```css
/* styles.css */

body {
    font-family: Arial, sans-serif;
    background-color: #f4f4f9;
    color: #333;
}

header {
    background-color: #4CAF50;
    color: white;
    padding: 20px;
    text-align: center;
}

main {
    margin: 20px;
    padding: 20px;
    background-color: white;
    border-radius: 8px;
}

button {
    padding: 10px 20px;
```

```
    background-color: #4CAF50;

    color: white;

    border: none;

    border-radius: 5px;

    cursor: pointer;

}


button:hover {

    background-color: #45a049;

}


footer {

    text-align: center;

    padding: 10px;

    background-color: #333;

    color: white;

}
```

- o **Explanation**:
  - body: Sets the general appearance of the webpage, such as font family and background color.
  - header: Styles the top section of the webpage, making it green with white text.
  - main: Adds padding and a white background to the content area.

38

- button: Customizes the appearance of the button, including padding, color, and hover effects.
- footer: Styles the footer with a dark background and white text.

With this structure, the page is visually appealing, and the content is well-organized. Now, JavaScript can manipulate these elements to add interactivity.

Adding JavaScript to HTML

JavaScript can be added to an HTML page in two primary ways: **inline** or **external**. For larger projects, it's best to use external JavaScript files.

1. **Inline JavaScript**: You can include JavaScript directly in the HTML file using the <script> tag:

```
html

<script>
    alert("Welcome    to    my    interactive
webpage!");
</script>
```

   o   This script will run as soon as the browser encounters the `<script>` tag.

2. **External JavaScript**: It's generally better to keep JavaScript code in separate files for easier management and debugging. To link an external JavaScript file, use the `<script>` tag at the end of your HTML file, right before the closing `</body>` tag:

```
html
```

```
<script src="app.js"></script>
```

   o   The `src` attribute points to the location of the external JavaScript file.

   o   **Why Add JavaScript at the End?** It's a good practice to place your JavaScript at the bottom of the HTML file so that the HTML content is fully loaded before the script runs. This prevents the browser from blocking rendering while JavaScript executes.

Real-World Example: Creating a Simple Interactive Web Page

Let's now put everything together to create a simple interactive webpage. In this example, we'll build a page with a button that changes text when clicked.

1. **HTML** **Structure**:

Create an HTML file called `index.html`:

html

```
<!DOCTYPE html>
<html lang="en">
<head>
    <meta charset="UTF-8">
    <meta                name="viewport"
content="width=device-width,      initial-
scale=1.0">
    <title>Interactive Web Page</title>
    <link               rel="stylesheet"
href="styles.css">
</head>
<body>
    <header>
        <h1>Interactive      Web      Page
Example</h1>
    </header>
    <main>
        <p   id="dynamicText">Click    the
button to change this text.</p>
        <button  id="changeTextBtn">Change
Text</button>
    </main>
    <footer>
        <p>© 2025 My Interactive Site</p>
```

```
  </footer>
  <script src="app.js"></script>
</body>
</html>
```

2. **CSS**   **Styling**:

Create a `styles.css` file:

```css
body {
    font-family: Arial, sans-serif;
    background-color: #f4f4f9;
    color: #333;
}

header {
    background-color: #4CAF50;
    color: white;
    padding: 20px;
    text-align: center;
}

main {
    margin: 20px;
    padding: 20px;
    background-color: white;
    border-radius: 8px;
}
```

```css
button {
    padding: 10px 20px;
    background-color: #4CAF50;
    color: white;
    border: none;
    border-radius: 5px;
    cursor: pointer;
}

button:hover {
    background-color: #45a049;
}

footer {
    text-align: center;
    padding: 10px;
    background-color: #333;
    color: white;
}
```

3. **JavaScript   Interactivity**:

Create a JavaScript file called app.js:

```javascript
document.getElementById('changeTextBtn').
addEventListener('click', function() {

document.getElementById('dynamicText').te
xtContent = 'The text has been changed!';
```

43

```
});
```

   o   This JavaScript code adds an event listener to the
       button. When the button is clicked, it changes the
       text inside the <p> tag with the id dynamicText.

Summary

In this chapter, you:

- Learned the relationship between **HTML**, **CSS**, and **JavaScript**, and how they work together to build web pages.
- Understood the basics of structuring HTML and styling it with CSS to create visually appealing pages.
- Discovered how to link external JavaScript files to your HTML and how to use JavaScript to add interactivity.
- Built a simple interactive web page that demonstrates how HTML, CSS, and JavaScript can work together to create engaging user experiences.

With this foundation, you're now equipped to start building more interactive and dynamic websites using the power of JavaScript alongside HTML and CSS.

CHAPTER 4

CORE JAVASCRIPT SYNTAX AND STRUCTURE

Variables, Data Types, and Operators

JavaScript is a dynamically typed language, which means that variables don't need to be explicitly declared with a type. You can assign values of different types to the same variable at any time. Let's dive into the basics of **variables**, **data types**, and **operators**.

1. **Variables**: In JavaScript, variables are containers for storing data values. There are three main ways to declare variables:

    o `var`: The traditional way of declaring variables. It's function-scoped, meaning it exists within the function where it's declared or globally if declared outside any function. However, `var` has some quirks that can lead to unintended behavior, so it's not recommended for modern JavaScript.

    o `let`: A more modern approach to variable declaration. It is block-scoped, which means it only exists within the block (e.g., inside curly

45

braces {}) in which it's declared. It's more predictable than `var`.

o `const`: Used for variables whose values should not change once assigned. It's also block-scoped.

Example:

```
javascript
```

```
let age = 25;  // Variable that can change
const birthYear = 1995;  // Constant value
that cannot be changed
```

2. **Data Types**: JavaScript has several built-in data types that allow you to store different kinds of data:

o **Primitive Types**:

- `Number`: Represents numeric values (e.g., 5, 3.14).

- `String`: Represents text (e.g., "Hello, World!").

- `Boolean`: Represents a true or false value (`true` or `false`).

- `Undefined`: Represents a variable that has not been assigned a value.

- `Null`: Represents the intentional absence of any value.

- Symbol: A unique and immutable value used primarily as object property keys.
- BigInt: Used to represent integers with arbitrary precision (e.g., 100n).

Example:

```javascript

let name = "John";  // String
let isStudent = true;  // Boolean
let score = 87.5;  // Number
let notAssigned;  // Undefined
let emptyValue = null;  // Null
```

3. **Operators**: Operators are symbols that perform operations on variables and values. Here are a few commonly used operators:

   o **Arithmetic Operators**: Used to perform mathematical operations.
     - +, -, *, /, % (modulus)
   o **Comparison Operators**: Used to compare values.
     - ==, ===, !=, >, <, >=, <=
   o **Logical Operators**: Used for logical operations.
     - && (AND), || (OR), ! (NOT)

Example:

47

```javascript
let a = 10;
let b = 5;
let result = a + b;   // Addition, result
will be 15
let isEqual = a == b;  // Comparison, result
will be false
```

Functions and Scope

1. **Functions**: A function is a block of code designed to perform a particular task. Functions help you avoid repeating code and make your program more modular and reusable.

   o **Declaring a Function**: Functions can be declared using the `function` keyword.

   o **Calling a Function**: Once declared, a function can be invoked (or called) using its name followed by parentheses.

Example:

```javascript
function greet(name) {
    console.log("Hello, " + name + "!");
}
```

```
greet("Alice");   // Calling the function,
output: Hello, Alice!
```

- o **Function Parameters and Return Values**: Functions can accept parameters (input) and return a value (output).

Example:

```javascript
javascript

function add(a, b) {
    return a + b;
}

let sum = add(5, 3);   // sum will be 8
```

2. **Scope**: In JavaScript, **scope** refers to the visibility and accessibility of variables. There are two main types of scope:
   - o **Global Scope**: Variables declared outside any function or block are in the global scope and are accessible from anywhere in the code.
   - o **Local Scope**: Variables declared inside a function or block are only accessible within that function or block. This is called **function scope** for var and **block scope** for let and const.

Example:

```javascript
let globalVar = "I am global";   // Global scope

function localScopeExample() {
    let localVar = "I am local";   // Local scope
    console.log(globalVar);   // Can access global variable
}

console.log(localVar);   // Error: localVar is not defined outside the function
```

Conditional Statements (if-else, switch-case)

1. **if-else Statement**: The `if` statement is used to make decisions in code. It checks a condition and, if true, executes a block of code.

    o **Syntax**:

    ```javascript
    if (condition) {
        // code to execute if condition is true
    ```

50

```
} else {
    // code to execute if condition
is false
}
```

2. **Example**:

3. javascript

4.

5. let age = 18;

6. if (age >= 18) {

7.   console.log("You are an adult.");

8. } else {

9.   console.log("You are a minor.");

10. }

11. **switch-case Statement**: The switch statement is used when you have multiple conditions to check against a single expression. It's a cleaner alternative to multiple if-else statements.

   o **Syntax**:

```
javascript

switch (expression) {
    case value1:
        // code to execute if
expression === value1
        break;
    case value2:
```

```
                    //   code    to   execute   if
expression === value2
            break;
        default:
            // code to execute if none of
the cases match
        }
```

12. **Example**:

```
13. javascript
14.
15. let day = 3;
16. switch (day) {
17.     case 1:
18.         console.log("Monday");
19.         break;
20.     case 2:
21.         console.log("Tuesday");
22.         break;
23.     case 3:
24.         console.log("Wednesday");
25.         break;
26.     default:
27.         console.log("Invalid day");
28. }
```

Real-world Example: A Dynamic Age Calculator

Let's build a simple age calculator that takes the user's birth year and calculates their current age. This will demonstrate how to use variables, functions, conditionals, and other concepts we've covered.

1. **HTML Structure**: Create an HTML file (`index.html`):

```html
html

<!DOCTYPE html>
<html lang="en">
<head>
    <meta charset="UTF-8">
    <meta                   name="viewport"
content="width=device-width,       initial-
scale=1.0">
    <title>Age Calculator</title>
</head>
<body>
    <h1>Dynamic Age Calculator</h1>
    <label   for="birthYear">Enter    your
birth year:</label>
    <input   type="number"   id="birthYear"
placeholder="e.g., 1990">
    <button    id="calculateBtn">Calculate
Age</button>
    <p id="result"></p>
```

```
      <script src="app.js"></script>
</body>
</html>
```

2. **CSS Styling** (styles.css):

```css
body {
    font-family: Arial, sans-serif;
    margin: 20px;
}

label {
    font-size: 18px;
}

input {
    padding: 5px;
    font-size: 16px;
}

button {
    padding: 10px 20px;
    background-color: #4CAF50;
    color: white;
    border: none;
    border-radius: 5px;
    cursor: pointer;
```

```
}

button:hover {
    background-color: #45a049;
}

#result {
    font-size: 20px;
    margin-top: 10px;
}
```

3. **JavaScript Code** (app.js):

javascript

```
document.getElementById('calculateBtn').a
ddEventListener('click', function() {
    let           birthYear           =
parseInt(document.getElementById('birthYe
ar').value);
    let      currentYear     =      new
Date().getFullYear();
    let age = currentYear - birthYear;

    if   (birthYear   >   currentYear   ||
birthYear < 1900) {

document.getElementById('result').textCon
tent = "Please enter a valid year.";
    } else {
```

```
document.getElementById('result').textCon
tent = `You are ${age} years old.`;
    }
});
```

Explanation:

- o   The user inputs their birth year, and upon clicking the "Calculate Age" button, JavaScript calculates their age based on the current year.
- o   If the entered year is invalid (e.g., future year or too old), the program displays an error message.
- o   The result is displayed dynamically on the webpage.

Summary

In this chapter, you:

- • Learned how to declare variables, work with different data types, and use operators to manipulate values in JavaScript.
- • Explored functions and scope to manage your code effectively and avoid errors.

- Understood how to use conditional statements (`if-else` and `switch-case`) to make decisions and control the flow of your program.
- Built a **Dynamic Age Calculator** to apply these concepts in a real-world example.

These foundational concepts form the building blocks of JavaScript programming, and mastering them will allow you to write dynamic and interactive web applications.

CHAPTER 5

WORKING WITH ARRAYS AND OBJECTS

Arrays: Creating, Accessing, and Manipulating Data

Arrays are one of the most powerful data structures in JavaScript. They allow you to store multiple values in a single variable and are useful for managing collections of data, such as lists, ordered items, or even complex datasets.

1. **Creating Arrays**: Arrays are created using square brackets `[]` and can hold any type of data, including numbers, strings, and objects. Elements in an array are indexed, meaning each value has a specific position (index) starting from 0.

   Example:

   ```javascript
   let fruits = ["apple", "banana", "cherry"];
   // Array of strings
   let numbers = [1, 2, 3, 4, 5];  // Array of
   numbers
   ```

```
let mixed = [1, "apple", true, null];   //
Array with mixed data types
```

2. **Accessing Array Elements**: You can access elements in an array by using their index. The index starts at 0, so the first element is at index 0, the second at index 1, and so on.

Example:

```
javascript
```

```
let fruits = ["apple", "banana", "cherry"];
console.log(fruits[0]);   // Output: apple
(first element)
console.log(fruits[2]);   // Output: cherry
(third element)
```

3. **Manipulating Arrays**: JavaScript provides several methods to manipulate arrays, such as adding, removing, and modifying elements.

   o **Push**: Adds an element to the end of an array.

   ```
   javascript
   ```

   ```
   fruits.push("orange");      //   Adds
   'orange' to the end of the array
   ```

```
console.log(fruits);    // Output:
['apple',    'banana',    'cherry',
'orange']
```

- o **Pop**: Removes the last element from an array.

  javascript

  ```
  fruits.pop();  // Removes 'orange'
  console.log(fruits);    // Output:
  ['apple', 'banana', 'cherry']
  ```

- o **Shift**: Removes the first element from an array.

  javascript

  ```
  fruits.shift();  // Removes 'apple'
  console.log(fruits);    // Output:
  ['banana', 'cherry']
  ```

- o **Unshift**: Adds an element to the beginning of the array.

  javascript

  ```
  fruits.unshift("kiwi");    // Adds
  'kiwi' to the beginning
  console.log(fruits);    // Output:
  ['kiwi', 'banana', 'cherry']
  ```

- o **Splice**: Adds/removes elements from anywhere in the array.

```javascript
fruits.splice(1, 1, "grape");    //
Removes 1 element at index 1 and adds
'grape'
console.log(fruits);    // Output:
['kiwi', 'grape', 'cherry']
```

- o **ForEach**: Loops through each element in an array.

```javascript
fruits.forEach(function(fruit) {
    console.log(fruit);  // Outputs
each fruit in the array
});
```

Objects: Structure and Use Cases

Objects are used to store collections of data and more complex entities. They are key-value pairs, where the key is a unique string (often referred to as a property) and the value can be any data type.

1. **Creating Objects**: You create objects using curly braces {} and assign properties with keys and values. The properties are separated by commas.

   Example:

```javascript
let person = {
    name: "John Doe",
    age: 30,
    job: "developer",
    isEmployed: true
};
```

2. **Accessing Object Properties**: You can access properties using dot notation or bracket notation.

   o **Dot Notation**:

```javascript
console.log(person.name);          //
Output: John Doe
console.log(person.age);  // Output:
30
```

   o **Bracket Notation**: This is useful when the property name is dynamic or contains special characters.

```
javascript
```

```
console.log(person["job"]);        //
Output: developer
```

3. **Adding or Modifying Object Properties**: You can add new properties or modify existing ones using dot or bracket notation.

   Example:

   ```
   javascript
   ```

   ```
   person.country = "USA";   // Adding a new
   property
   person.age = 31;  // Modifying an existing
   property
   console.log(person);   // Output: { name:
   "John Doe", age: 31, job: "developer",
   isEmployed: true, country: "USA" }
   ```

4. **Deleting Object Properties**: To delete a property from an object, use the `delete` keyword.

   ```
   javascript
   ```

   ```
   delete person.isEmployed;   // Removes the
   'isEmployed' property
   ```

```
console.log(person);     // Output: { name:
"John  Doe",  age:  31,  job:  "developer",
country: "USA" }
```

5. **Nested Objects**: Objects can also contain other objects, creating a nested structure.

Example:

```javascript

let person = {
    name: "John Doe",
    address: {
        street: "123 Main St",
        city: "New York",
        zip: "10001"
    }
};
console.log(person.address.city);        //
Output: New York
```

Real-world Example: Creating a Simple To-Do List App

In this real-world example, we'll build a simple To-Do List app using both arrays and objects. The app will allow users to add, remove, and mark tasks as complete.

1. **HTML Structure**: Create a file called index.html:

64

html

```html
<!DOCTYPE html>
<html lang="en">
<head>
    <meta charset="UTF-8">
    <meta              name="viewport"
content="width=device-width,     initial-
scale=1.0">
    <title>To-Do List App</title>
    <link              rel="stylesheet"
href="styles.css">
</head>
<body>
    <h1>My To-Do List</h1>
    <input   type="text"   id="taskInput"
placeholder="Add a new task">
    <button         id="addTaskBtn">Add
Task</button>

    <ul id="taskList"></ul>

    <script src="app.js"></script>
</body>
</html>
```

2. **CSS Styling** (styles.css):

css

```css
body {
    font-family: Arial, sans-serif;
    margin: 20px;
}

input, button {
    padding: 10px;
    margin: 10px;
    font-size: 16px;
}

ul {
    list-style-type: none;
    padding: 0;
}

li {
    background-color: #f4f4f4;
    padding: 10px;
    margin: 5px 0;
    display: flex;
    justify-content: space-between;
    align-items: center;
}

li.completed {
    text-decoration: line-through;
    background-color: #d3ffd3;
}
```

```css
button.delete {
    background-color: red;
    color: white;
    border: none;
    cursor: pointer;
}

button.delete:hover {
    background-color: #cc0000;
}
```

3. **JavaScript Code** (app.js):

```javascript
javascript

let tasks = [];  // Array to hold tasks

// Task constructor (Object)
function Task(description) {
    this.description = description;
    this.completed = false;
}

// Add task to the array
document.getElementById('addTaskBtn').add
EventListener('click', function() {
    let          taskInput          =
document.getElementById('taskInput').valu
e;
```

```
    if (taskInput) {
        let newTask = new Task(taskInput);
        tasks.push(newTask);
        displayTasks();

document.getElementById('taskInput').valu
e = '';  // Clear the input field
    }
});

// Display all tasks
function displayTasks() {
    let         taskList         =
document.getElementById('taskList');
    taskList.innerHTML = '';  // Clear the
list before displaying the updated tasks
    tasks.forEach((task, index) => {
        let         li         =
document.createElement('li');
        li.classList.toggle('completed',
task.completed);
        li.innerHTML = `
            ${task.description}
            <button         class="delete"
onclick="deleteTask(${index})">Delete</bu
tton>
            <button
onclick="toggleCompletion(${index})">${ta
```

```
sk.completed          ?          'Undo'          :
'Complete'}</button>
        `;
        taskList.appendChild(li);
    });
}


// Toggle task completion
function toggleCompletion(index) {
    tasks[index].completed          =
!tasks[index].completed;
    displayTasks();
}


// Delete task
function deleteTask(index) {
    tasks.splice(index, 1);
    displayTasks();
}
```

Explanation:

- o **Task Object**: We define a `Task` constructor
  function to create objects with properties
  `description` and `completed`.

- o **Adding Tasks**: When the user clicks the "Add
  Task" button, the `Task` object is created and
  added to the `tasks` array.

- o **Displaying Tasks**: The tasks are displayed in an unordered list (`<ul>`), with each task having buttons to mark it as complete or delete it.

- o **Marking as Complete**: Clicking the "Complete" button toggles the task's completion status, and tasks that are completed are styled with a line-through.

- o **Deleting Tasks**: Clicking the "Delete" button removes the task from the array.

Summary

In this chapter, you:

- Learned how to work with **arrays** to store and manipulate ordered data.
- Explored **objects**, which are essential for managing structured data with properties and methods.
- Created a real-world example, a **To-Do List app**, that demonstrates the power of arrays and objects to manage tasks in an interactive web application.

These concepts are fundamental to JavaScript development and will help you build more complex applications as you continue learning. Arrays and objects are the building blocks of data management in JavaScript and are used in virtually every JavaScript project you'll undertake.

CHAPTER 6

LOOPS AND ITERATION TECHNIQUES

For Loop, While Loop, and Do-While Loop

Loops are essential for repeating a block of code multiple times. They are commonly used to iterate over collections (like arrays) and perform tasks multiple times without writing repetitive code. In JavaScript, we have several types of loops that allow us to control the flow of iterations.

1. **For Loop**: The `for` loop is one of the most commonly used loops in JavaScript. It runs a block of code for a specified number of iterations. The syntax is as follows:

```javascript

for (initialization; condition; increment)
{
    // code to be executed
}
```

- o **Initialization**: Typically used to define and set the starting point of a counter variable.

- o **Condition**: Specifies the condition that must be true for the loop to run.
- o **Increment**: Updates the counter variable after each iteration.

Example:

javascript

```
for (let i = 0; i < 5; i++) {
    console.log(i);  // Output: 0, 1, 2, 3,
4
}
```

2. **While Loop**: A `while` loop repeats a block of code as long as a specified condition is true. The condition is evaluated before each iteration.

javascript

```
while (condition) {
    // code to be executed
}
```

Example:

javascript

```
let i = 0;
```

```
while (i < 5) {
    console.log(i);  // Output: 0, 1, 2, 3,
4
    i++;
}
```

- o The loop will continue until the condition evaluates to false.
- o If the condition is initially false, the code inside the loop will never execute.

3. **Do-While Loop**: The `do-while` loop is similar to the `while` loop, except that the condition is evaluated after the loop's body is executed. This guarantees that the loop's code runs at least once, even if the condition is initially false.

javascript

```
do {
    // code to be executed
} while (condition);
```

Example:

javascript

```
let i = 0;
do {
```

```
    console.log(i);  // Output: 0, 1, 2, 3,
4
    i++;
} while (i < 5);
```

- o The key difference is that the loop will always run at least once, regardless of the condition's truth value.

Advanced Iteration: map(), filter(), and reduce()

In addition to traditional loops, JavaScript provides powerful array methods like `map()`, `filter()`, and `reduce()` that allow you to iterate over data in a more functional and concise way.

1. **map()**: The `map()` method creates a new array populated with the results of calling a provided function on every element in the array. It doesn't modify the original array.

   Syntax:

   ```javascript
   let              newArray          =
   array.map(function(currentValue,    index,
   array) {
       // Return the new value
   });
   ```

75

Example:

javascript

```
let numbers = [1, 2, 3, 4];
let doubled = numbers.map(function(number)
{
    return number * 2;
});
console.log(doubled);  // Output: [2, 4, 6,
8]
```

- o   map() is useful when you need to transform each element in an array and return a new array with the transformed values.

2. **filter()**: The filter() method creates a new array with all elements that pass the test implemented by the provided function. It filters out elements that don't meet the condition.

Syntax:

javascript

```
let             newArray             =
array.filter(function(currentValue, index,
array) {
    //   Return   true   or   false   to
include/exclude element
```

```
});
```

Example:

```
javascript

let numbers = [1, 2, 3, 4, 5];
let           evenNumbers         =
numbers.filter(function(number) {
    return number % 2 === 0;
});
console.log(evenNumbers);   // Output: [2,
4]
```

- o `filter()` is helpful when you want to create a new array with only the elements that meet certain criteria.

3. **reduce()**: The `reduce()` method executes a reducer function (provided by you) on each element of the array, resulting in a single output value. It is often used to sum values, calculate averages, or combine array elements.

Syntax:

```
javascript

let           result         =
array.reduce(function(accumulator,
currentValue, index, array) {
```

```
        // Return the updated accumulator value
}, initialValue);
```

Example:

```javascript

let numbers = [1, 2, 3, 4];
let sum = numbers.reduce(function(acc,
current) {
    return acc + current;
}, 0);
console.log(sum);   // Output: 10
```

- o   reduce() is very powerful for accumulating values or performing complex transformations on arrays.

Real-world Example: Building a List of Dynamic Items

Let's now apply the concepts of loops, iteration techniques, and JavaScript functions to create a simple interactive to-do list app. This app will allow users to add tasks dynamically, display them in a list, and remove tasks when they're completed.

1. **HTML Structure**: Create an index.html file:

```
html
```

```
<!DOCTYPE html>
<html lang="en">
<head>
    <meta charset="UTF-8">
    <meta                name="viewport"
content="width=device-width,      initial-
scale=1.0">
    <title>Dynamic To-Do List</title>
    <link              rel="stylesheet"
href="styles.css">
</head>
<body>
    <h1>To-Do List</h1>
    <input    type="text"    id="taskInput"
placeholder="Add a new task">
    <button          id="addTaskBtn">Add
Task</button>
    <ul id="taskList"></ul>

    <script src="app.js"></script>
</body>
</html>
```

2. **CSS Styling** (styles.css):

```css
css


body {
    font-family: Arial, sans-serif;
```

79

```css
    margin: 20px;
}

input, button {
    padding: 10px;
    font-size: 16px;
}

ul {
    list-style-type: none;
    padding: 0;
}

li {
    padding: 10px;
    margin: 5px 0;
    background-color: #f4f4f4;
    display: flex;
    justify-content: space-between;
    align-items: center;
}

button.delete {
    background-color: red;
    color: white;
    border: none;
    cursor: pointer;
}
```

```css
button.delete:hover {
    background-color: darkred;
}
```

3. **JavaScript Code** (app.js):

```javascript
javascript

let tasks = [];  // Array to store tasks

// Add task function
document.getElementById('addTaskBtn').add
EventListener('click', function() {
    let           taskInput           =
document.getElementById('taskInput').valu
e;
    if (taskInput) {
        tasks.push({    task:    taskInput,
completed: false });  // Add new task to
array
        displayTasks();

document.getElementById('taskInput').valu
e = '';  // Clear input field
    }
});

// Display tasks function
function displayTasks() {
```

```javascript
    let           taskList          =
document.getElementById('taskList');
    taskList.innerHTML = '';    // Clear
current task list before displaying updated
tasks

    // Loop through tasks array and display
each task
    tasks.forEach(function(task, index) {
        let            li           =
document.createElement('li');
        li.classList.toggle('completed',
task.completed);
        li.innerHTML = `
            ${task.task}
            <button          class="delete"
onclick="deleteTask(${index})">Delete</bu
tton>
            <button
onclick="toggleCompletion(${index})">${ta
sk.completed      ?      'Undo'       :
'Complete'}</button>
            `;
        taskList.appendChild(li);
    });
}

// Toggle task completion
function toggleCompletion(index) {
```

```
    tasks[index].completed          =
!tasks[index].completed;        //    Toggle
completion status
    displayTasks();
}


// Delete task
function deleteTask(index) {
    tasks.splice(index, 1); // Remove task
from array
    displayTasks();
}
```

Explanation:

- o **tasks Array**: Stores the tasks as objects, where each object has a `task` property (task description) and a `completed` property (true or false).

- o **displayTasks()**: This function loops through the `tasks` array and displays each task in an unordered list (`<ul>`). It uses a `forEach()` loop to iterate over the array and create a list item (`<li>`) for each task.

- o **toggleCompletion()**: Allows the user to mark a task as complete or incomplete.

- o **deleteTask()**: Deletes a task from the array when the delete button is clicked.

83

Summary

In this chapter, you:

- Learned how to use **for loops**, **while loops**, and **do-while loops** to iterate over data.
- Explored advanced iteration techniques like **map()**, **filter()**, and **reduce()**, which provide more functional ways to manipulate arrays.
- Built a **dynamic to-do list app** that utilizes loops and array methods to add, delete, and mark tasks as complete, providing hands-on practice with iteration.

These techniques are fundamental when working with dynamic data, and mastering them will help you write efficient and concise code for interactive web applications.

CHAPTER 7

ERROR HANDLING AND DEBUGGING TECHNIQUES

Using try-catch for Error Handling

In JavaScript, errors can occur for various reasons, such as incorrect data types, missing files, or network issues. It's essential to handle these errors gracefully to prevent your application from crashing unexpectedly. The **try-catch** statement is a mechanism for handling errors, allowing you to control the flow of your program even when errors occur.

1. **Syntax of try-catch**: The basic syntax of the `try-catch` statement is:

```javascript
try {
    // Code that may throw an error
} catch (error) {
    // Code to handle the error
}
```

- o The **try** block contains the code that may cause an error.
- o The **catch** block handles the error if one occurs. It captures the error in a variable (commonly named error or e).

2. **Example of try-catch**: Let's consider a simple example where we try to convert a string to a number and catch any errors that may occur during the conversion:

javascript

```
try {
    let userInput = "Hello";
    let number = parseInt(userInput);
    if (isNaN(number)) {
        throw new Error("Input is not a
valid number!");
    }
    console.log(number);
} catch (error) {
    console.log("Error:", error.message);
// Output: Error: Input is not a valid
number!
}
```

- o The **throw** statement allows you to generate a custom error. In the example, we check if the

86

input is a valid number, and if not, we throw an error with a message.

3. **Finally Block**: JavaScript also supports a **finally** block, which is always executed after the try and catch blocks, regardless of whether an error occurred or not. It is typically used for cleanup actions.

```javascript
try {
    let result = riskyFunction();
} catch (error) {
    console.log("An    error    occurred:",
error.message);
} finally {
    console.log("Cleaning                up
resources...");  // This always runs
}
```

o   The **finally** block is helpful when you need to ensure that some cleanup code runs (like closing a file, releasing resources, etc.), regardless of the success or failure of the try block.

Debugging Tools and Techniques

Debugging is an essential skill for identifying and fixing issues in your code. There are several tools and techniques you can use to debug JavaScript applications.

1. **Console Logging**: One of the simplest debugging techniques is to use `console.log()` to print variable values and trace the flow of execution.

   o **Example**:

   ```javascript
   let userAge = 25;
   console.log("User Age:", userAge);
   ```

   You can use `console.log()` to print out values at various points in your program to check if everything is working as expected.

   o **Other Console Methods**:

   - `console.error()`: Logs an error message.
   - `console.warn()`: Logs a warning message.
   - `console.table()`: Logs data in a table format.

- `console.assert()`: Throws an error if the condition is false.

Example:

```
javascript

console.warn("This is a warning!");
console.error("This    is    an    error
message!");
```

2. **Breakpoints and Debugging in Developer Tools**: Modern web browsers, like Google Chrome, come with built-in developer tools (DevTools) that provide powerful debugging features. You can use **breakpoints** to pause the execution of your JavaScript code at a specific line and inspect the variables and call stack.

   o **Steps to Use Breakpoints** in Chrome DevTools:

      1. Open **DevTools** by pressing `F12` or right-clicking on the page and selecting **Inspect**.

      2. Go to the **Sources** tab.

      3. Open the JavaScript file you want to debug.

      4. Click on the line number where you want to set a breakpoint.

      5. Reload the page or trigger the function, and the code will pause at the breakpoint.

    o   You can also use **watch expressions** to keep track of specific variables and see their values in real time.

3. **Using the Debugger Statement**: JavaScript provides a built-in `debugger` statement that works similarly to setting breakpoints in DevTools. When the `debugger` statement is executed, the code will pause, and the developer tools will open, allowing you to inspect the state.

Example:

```javascript

function testFunction() {
    let x = 5;
    debugger;  // Execution will pause here
    console.log(x);
}


testFunction();
```

    o   When the `debugger` statement is encountered, the browser will automatically pause the execution, allowing you to inspect the variables and execution flow.

4. **Using Linters**: **Linters** are tools that analyze your code for potential errors and stylistic issues before runtime.

90

Tools like **ESLint** can catch syntax errors, unused variables, and other common mistakes as you write your code.

○ To use ESLint in your project, install it via npm:

```bash
npm install eslint --save-dev
```

○ You can then set up ESLint and configure it to your needs, or use a pre-built configuration to check your code for errors.

Real-world Example: Debugging a JavaScript Application

Let's consider a simple application where we calculate the total price of items in a shopping cart. We will intentionally introduce an error and then debug it using various techniques.

1. **HTML Structure** (`index.html`):

```html
<!DOCTYPE html>
<html lang="en">
<head>
    <meta charset="UTF-8">
```

```
    <meta                name="viewport"
content="width=device-width,     initial-
scale=1.0">
    <title>Shopping Cart</title>
</head>
<body>
    <h1>Shopping Cart</h1>
    <p id="totalPrice"></p>
    <script src="app.js"></script>
</body>
</html>
```

2. **JavaScript Code** (app.js):

```javascript
javascript

let cart = [
    { name: "Item 1", price: 10 },
    { name: "Item 2", price: 20 },
    { name: "Item 3", price: 30 }
];

function calculateTotal() {
    let total = 0;
    for (let i = 0; i < cart.length; i++)
{
        total += cart[i].price;
    }
    return total;
}
```

```
let totalPrice = calculateTotal();
console.log("Total  Price:",  totalPrice);
// Debugging step

// Simulate an error in displaying the
total price
document.getElementById('totalPrice').tex
tContent  =  totalPrices;   // Mistake:
incorrect variable name
```

3. **Error in the Code**: There is a typo in the code where the `totalPrice` variable is used in the `textContent` assignment. The variable is incorrectly referenced as `totalPrices` (plural).

4. **Debugging the Error**: Let's debug this using different techniques:

   o **Step 1**: Use `console.log()` to check the value of `totalPrice`:

   ```javascript
   ```

   ```
   console.log("Total       Price:",
   totalPrice);  // This will output:
   Total Price: 60
   ```

   o **Step 2**: Check the browser console for any errors: When you run the application, the browser will show an error like:

```csharp
Uncaught ReferenceError: totalPrices
is not defined
```

- o **Step 3**: Using Chrome Developer Tools:
    1. Open DevTools by pressing `F12` or right-clicking and selecting **Inspect**.
    2. Go to the **Console** tab, where the error message appears.
    3. Inspect the variables and see that `totalPrices` is the incorrect reference.
- o **Step 4**: Fix the error: Change the typo from `totalPrices` to `totalPrice`:

```javascript
document.getElementById('totalPrice').textContent = totalPrice;    // Corrected line
```

5. **Result**: After fixing the error, the total price will correctly be displayed on the page:

```yaml
Total Price: 60
```

Summary

In this chapter, you:

- Learned how to handle errors in JavaScript using `try-catch` to catch exceptions and provide meaningful error messages.
- Explored **debugging techniques**, including **console logging**, **breakpoints**, and **DevTools**, to identify and fix issues in your code.
- Walked through a **real-world example** of debugging a shopping cart application, where we identified and resolved an error using various debugging strategies.

Effective error handling and debugging are essential for building robust and reliable JavaScript applications. By mastering these techniques, you'll be able to identify, troubleshoot, and fix issues quickly and efficiently.

CHAPTER 8

ADVANCED FUNCTIONS AND CLOSURES

Understanding Functions and Scope in Depth

In JavaScript, functions are essential building blocks of code. They allow you to group statements together, perform calculations, and manipulate data in a modular and reusable way. Understanding **functions** and **scope** is crucial to writing effective JavaScript code.

1. **Function Declaration**: Functions in JavaScript are declared using the `function` keyword followed by a name and parameters (optional). The body of the function contains the code to execute.

   Syntax:

   ```
   javascript

   function functionName(parameters) {
       // Code to execute
   }
   ```

Example:

```javascript
javascript

function greet(name) {
    console.log("Hello, " + name + "!");
}

greet("Alice");   // Output: Hello, Alice!
```

2. **Parameters and Arguments**:
   - o **Parameters** are placeholders used in function definitions to define what values the function expects.
   - o **Arguments** are the actual values passed into the function when it's called.

Example:

```javascript
javascript

function sum(a, b) {
    return a + b;
}

console.log(sum(3, 5));   // Output: 8
```

97

3. **Scope in JavaScript**: Scope refers to the accessibility or visibility of variables. JavaScript has two primary types of scope:

   o **Global Scope**: Variables declared outside any function are in the global scope and are accessible throughout the entire code.

   o **Local Scope**: Variables declared inside a function are in the local scope and are only accessible within that function.

Example:

```javascript

let globalVar = "I am global";  // Global scope

function localScope() {
    let localVar = "I am local";  // Local scope
    console.log(globalVar);  // Can access global variable
    console.log(localVar);  // Can access local variable
}

localScope();
console.log(globalVar);  // Output: I am global
```

```
//  console.log(localVar);      //  Error:
localVar is not defined
```

JavaScript's **lexical scope** means that functions are able to access variables from the surrounding scope in which they were defined, even if they are called from another scope.

Closures and How They Work

A **closure** is a function that has access to its own scope, the scope in which it was defined, and the global scope. Closures are created every time a function is defined, and they allow functions to "remember" and access variables from their outer scope, even after that outer function has finished executing.

1. **What is a Closure?**: A closure is formed when a function is created inside another function, and the inner function **"remembers"** the variables from its outer function's scope even after the outer function has returned. This allows the inner function to continue to access those variables.

2. **Why are Closures Useful?**: Closures are particularly useful for creating **data privacy** and **encapsulation**. They allow you to create functions with private data that cannot be directly accessed from the outside.

3. **Syntax of Closures**:

99

o   The outer function creates a local scope.

o   The inner function has access to the variables from the outer function.

o   Even after the outer function has finished executing, the inner function can still access the outer function's variables.

Example:

javascript

```
function outerFunction(outerVar) {
    return                      function
innerFunction(innerVar) {
        console.log(outerVar);    // Inner
function has access to outerVar
        console.log(innerVar);    // Inner
function has access to innerVar
    };
}


let          closureExample          =
outerFunction("Outer");   // outerFunction
is executed
closureExample("Inner");       //   Output:
Outer, Inner
```

o   In the above example, innerFunction is a closure because it "remembers" the value of `outerVar` even after `outerFunction` has returned.

4. **Practical Uses of Closures**:

   o **Private Variables**: Closures allow you to create private data that cannot be accessed or modified from outside the function.

   o **Function Factories**: Closures can be used to create functions with pre-configured settings.

Real-world Example: Creating a Counter with Closures

Let's look at a real-world example to understand how closures can be used in practice. In this example, we will create a counter that can increment, decrement, and reset, all while maintaining the state (the counter value) privately.

1. **HTML Structure**: This example will be purely JavaScript-based to demonstrate closures, but we can also integrate it with an HTML interface later.

2. **JavaScript Code** (`app.js`):

```javascript

function createCounter() {
    let count = 0;  // This is a private
variable, accessible only within the
closure
```

101

```javascript
    // Return an object with methods to
modify and access the private count
variable
    return {
        increment: function() {
            count++;
            console.log("Count:", count);
        },
        decrement: function() {
            count--;
            console.log("Count:", count);
        },
        reset: function() {
            count = 0;
            console.log("Count     reset:",
count);
        }
    };
}

// Creating a counter instance
let counter = createCounter();

// Using the counter's methods
counter.increment();  // Output: Count: 1
counter.increment();  // Output: Count: 2
counter.decrement();  // Output: Count: 1
```

```
counter.reset();          // Output: Count
reset: 0
```

Explanation:

- o **createCounter()** is a function that returns an object containing three methods: `increment()`, `decrement()`, and `reset()`.
- o These methods can access the **private variable count** because they are closures, meaning they "remember" the scope of `createCounter()`, even after it has finished executing.
- o **Encapsulation**: The counter value is private to the `createCounter()` function, and you can only change it through the methods provided by the returned object.

This example demonstrates how closures can be used to create a counter with private state, ensuring that the count value cannot be accessed or modified directly from outside the function.

Summary

In this chapter, you:

- Gained a deeper understanding of **functions** and **scope**, learning about the different types of function declarations, parameter handling, and how scope impacts variable accessibility.
- Explored **closures**, understanding how they allow inner functions to "remember" and access variables from their outer scope, even after the outer function has completed execution.
- Built a **counter application** using closures, which demonstrated how closures can be used to create private data and function factories.

Mastering closures is crucial for writing modular, maintainable, and secure JavaScript code. Understanding how closures work will help you create more complex functions with hidden internal states, useful for scenarios such as private data management, event handling, and creating reusable code patterns.

CHAPTER 9

ASYNCHRONOUS JAVASCRIPT AND CALLBACKS

The Need for Asynchronous Code in Web Development

In modern web development, asynchronous programming is a critical concept. It allows web applications to remain responsive and perform non-blocking operations, such as making API calls, loading resources, or interacting with databases, without freezing the user interface.

1. **What is Asynchronous Code?** Asynchronous code allows the execution of tasks to proceed without blocking the rest of the code from running. In synchronous code, each line of code is executed one after the other, blocking the program until each task is completed. However, with asynchronous code, operations like data fetching or file reading can happen in the background while the rest of the application remains interactive.

   Why is Asynchronous Code Necessary?

- o **User Experience**: Asynchronous operations keep the user interface responsive, even when waiting for time-consuming tasks like network requests or file downloads.

- o **Performance**: Asynchronous code can help avoid unnecessary delays in the execution of tasks, which leads to faster and more efficient web applications.

Example: Without asynchronous programming, if you had to fetch data from a server, the entire page would freeze until the request was completed, making it impossible for users to interact with the page. Asynchronous code allows the rest of the page to continue functioning while the data is being fetched in the background.

2. **How Does Asynchronous JavaScript Work?** Asynchronous tasks are typically handled using **callbacks**, **Promises**, or **async/await**. In this chapter, we'll focus on callbacks, which are one of the oldest and most widely used mechanisms for handling asynchronous code in JavaScript.

Using Callbacks to Handle Asynchronous Code

A **callback** is a function that is passed into another function as an argument and is executed after the completion of a task or event. Callbacks are used to handle asynchronous code and allow a function to be executed once an asynchronous operation is complete.

1. **Basic Structure of a Callback**:
   - o You define a function that performs an asynchronous operation (like fetching data or waiting for a timeout).
   - o Once the asynchronous task is completed, you call the callback function to handle the result.

Syntax:

```javascript
function someAsyncOperation(callback) {
    // Simulating asynchronous task
    setTimeout(() => {
        callback("Task Complete");
    }, 2000);   // Executes the callback after 2 seconds
}

// Callback function
function handleResult(message) {
```

107

```
        console.log(message);
}


// Calling the function with the callback
someAsyncOperation(handleResult);          //
Output: Task Complete (after 2 seconds)
```

2. **Callback Functions in Asynchronous Code**: Callbacks are commonly used in JavaScript for tasks like reading files, making HTTP requests, or handling events.

   o **setTimeout()**: Executes a function after a specified time interval (in milliseconds).

   o **setInterval()**: Repeatedly calls a function at specified intervals.

   o **Event Listeners**: Callbacks can be passed as event handlers for DOM events (e.g., `click`, `submit`).

Example of `setTimeout()`:

```javascript
console.log("Start");

setTimeout(() => {
    console.log("This    runs    after    3
seconds");
}, 3000);
```

```
console.log("End");
```

- o **Output**:

```
pgsql
```

```
Start
End
This runs after 3 seconds
```

Even though the `setTimeout` function waits for 3 seconds, it does not block the program from running the other parts of the code.

3. **Handling Errors in Callbacks**: One common issue when working with callbacks is handling errors. It's a good practice to pass an error as the first argument to the callback function. This is known as **error-first callbacks**.

Example:

```javascript
function fetchData(callback) {
    let success = true;

    if (success) {
        callback(null,    "Data    fetched
successfully");
```

```
      } else {
          callback("Error   fetching   data",
null);
      }
  }

  fetchData(function(error, data) {
      if (error) {
          console.error(error);
      } else {
          console.log(data);
      }
  });
```

In the example, the callback receives an error message or the result, depending on the success or failure of the operation.

Real-world Example: Creating a Polling System

A **polling system** is an example of asynchronous programming in real-time applications. It repeatedly checks for new data from the server at regular intervals. Let's create a simple polling system that fetches the latest data every few seconds.

1. **HTML Structure** (index.html):

```
html
```

```
<!DOCTYPE html>
<html lang="en">
<head>
    <meta charset="UTF-8">
    <meta                   name="viewport"
content="width=device-width,      initial-
scale=1.0">
    <title>Polling System Example</title>
</head>
<body>
    <h1>Latest Server Data</h1>
    <div id="dataDisplay"></div>

    <script src="app.js"></script>
</body>
</html>
```

2. **JavaScript Code** (app.js): In this example, we simulate fetching data from the server using setInterval(). Every 5 seconds, the polling function checks for new data.

```javascript
function fetchServerData(callback) {
    // Simulate an asynchronous request
(e.g., fetching from a server)
    setTimeout(() => {
        let data = {
```

111

```
            message:   "New   data   fetched
from the server",
            timestamp:                   new
Date().toLocaleTimeString()
        };
        callback(null, data);  // No error,
data returned
    }, 2000);  // Simulate a 2-second delay
for the request
}


function displayData(error, data) {
    if (error) {
        console.error("Error:", error);
        return;
    }
    const          displayElement         =
document.getElementById("dataDisplay");
    displayElement.innerHTML = `
        <p>${data.message}</p>
        <p>Last                    updated:
${data.timestamp}</p>
    `;
}


// Polling every 5 seconds (5000 ms)
setInterval(() => {
    console.log("Checking      for      new
data...");
```

112

```
        fetchServerData(displayData);
}, 5000);
```

3. **Explanation**:

   o The `fetchServerData()` function simulates an asynchronous request to the server using `setTimeout()`. After 2 seconds, it calls the callback function (`displayData`) with the fetched data.

   o The `displayData()` function receives the data and updates the content on the web page by changing the inner HTML of the `#dataDisplay` element.

   o The `setInterval()` function is used to call `fetchServerData()` every 5 seconds, simulating a real-time polling system.

4. **How it Works**:

   o Every 5 seconds, the `fetchServerData()` function is called.

   o The server data is simulated with a message and timestamp, and the `displayData()` function updates the HTML with the latest information.

   o The system continues to fetch and display the latest data every 5 seconds without blocking the user interface.

   Example Output:

```
sql

Checking for new data...
(After 2 seconds)
New data fetched from the server
Last updated: 12:15:30 PM
```

Summary

In this chapter, you:

- Learned the importance of **asynchronous programming** for keeping web applications responsive and efficient.
- Explored **callbacks**, which allow JavaScript to handle asynchronous tasks by executing a function after an operation completes.
- Built a **polling system** to simulate fetching data from a server at regular intervals using asynchronous techniques like setTimeout() and setInterval().

Asynchronous programming and callbacks are fundamental to modern web development, allowing you to handle time-consuming operations (like fetching data or waiting for user input) without freezing the user interface. By mastering these concepts, you can create more dynamic and interactive web applications.

CHAPTER 10

PROMISES AND ASYNC/AWAIT

Promises: Solving Callback Hell

One of the biggest challenges in JavaScript when dealing with asynchronous code is **callback hell** (also known as **pyramid of doom**). This happens when multiple nested callbacks are used, leading to code that is difficult to read, understand, and maintain.

1. **What are Promises?** A **Promise** is an object representing the eventual completion or failure of an asynchronous operation. It allows you to attach handlers to handle both success (`resolve`) and failure (`reject`) cases. Promises provide a cleaner, more readable way to work with asynchronous code compared to callbacks.

   Promise States:

   o **Pending**: The promise is still being executed (i.e., the asynchronous operation is still in progress).

   o **Resolved**: The asynchronous operation was successful, and the promise has been fulfilled with a result.

115

    o **Rejected**: The asynchronous operation failed, and the promise was rejected with an error.

2. **Promise Syntax**: A promise is created using the `new Promise()` constructor, which takes a function with two parameters: `resolve` and `reject`.

Syntax:

```javascript
let promise = new Promise((resolve, reject) => {
    // Asynchronous code
    if (/* success condition */) {
        resolve(result);          //      If
successful, call resolve() with the result
    } else {
        reject(error);  // If failed, call
reject() with an error
    }
});
```

Example:

```javascript
let myPromise = new Promise((resolve, reject) => {
    let isSuccess = true;
```

```
    if (isSuccess) {
        resolve("The      operation      was
successful!");
    } else {
        reject("The operation failed.");
    }
});


myPromise
    .then(result => {
        console.log(result);    // Output:
The operation was successful!
    })
    .catch(error => {
        console.log(error);         //    If
rejected, output the error
    });
```

- o **then()**: A method that takes a function to handle the result of a resolved promise.
- o **catch()**: A method that handles the error if the promise is rejected.

3. **Chaining Promises**: Promises can be chained using multiple .then() methods. This allows you to execute asynchronous operations sequentially in a clean manner, avoiding callback hell.

Example:

```javascript

let myPromise = new Promise((resolve,
reject) => {
    setTimeout(() => resolve("First step
completed"), 1000);
});

myPromise
    .then(result => {
        console.log(result);    // Output:
First step completed
        return new Promise((resolve,
reject) => {
            setTimeout(()                    =>
resolve("Second step completed"), 1000);
        });
    })
    .then(result => {
        console.log(result);    // Output:
Second step completed
    })
    .catch(error => {
        console.log(error);    // If any
promise is rejected
    });
```

- o Each `.then()` returns a new promise, allowing
    for sequential asynchronous tasks. If any promise

in the chain fails, the error is caught by `.catch()`.

Async/Await for Clean Asynchronous Code

async and **await** are new keywords introduced in ES8 (ES2017) that simplify working with asynchronous code. They are built on top of Promises, making asynchronous code look and behave more like synchronous code, which is easier to read and debug.

1. **What is async?** The `async` keyword is used to declare a function as asynchronous. An `async` function always returns a Promise, and inside an `async` function, you can use the `await` keyword to pause execution until a Promise is resolved.

2. **What is await?** The `await` keyword can only be used inside an `async` function. It makes JavaScript wait for the Promise to resolve or reject before moving on to the next line of code.

Syntax:

```javascript
async function myFunction() {
    let result = await somePromise;
```

```
console.log(result);  // This waits for
the promise to resolve
}
```

3. **Example Using `async` and `await`**:

```javascript
function fetchData() {
    return new Promise((resolve, reject)
=> {
        setTimeout(() => {
            resolve("Data          fetched
successfully!");
        }, 2000);
    });
}

async function displayData() {
    console.log("Fetching data...");
    let data = await fetchData();  // Waits
for the promise to resolve
    console.log(data);    // Output: Data
fetched successfully!
}

displayData();
```

   o In this example, `await fetchData()` pauses
      execution until `fetchData()` resolves, making

the code look like it's executing synchronously, even though it's still asynchronous.

4. **Handling Errors with `try-catch`**: When using async/await, errors are typically handled using try-catch blocks, making it easier to work with errors in asynchronous code.

Example:

javascript

```
async function fetchData() {
    throw new Error("Something went wrong!");
}

async function displayData() {
    try {
        let data = await fetchData();
        console.log(data);
    } catch (error) {
        console.log("Error:", error.message);    // Output: Error: Something went wrong!
    }
}

displayData();
```

- o The `try` block allows you to execute the asynchronous code, and the `catch` block catches any errors that might occur during the execution.

Real-world Example: Fetching Data from an API

Let's create an example where we use `async/await` to fetch data from an API. We'll simulate fetching data from a public API (such as a JSON placeholder API) and display the result.

1. **Example Setup**:
   - o We will fetch a list of users from a public API, process the response, and display the names of users in a list format.
2. **HTML Structure** (`index.html`):

```html

<!DOCTYPE html>
<html lang="en">
<head>
    <meta charset="UTF-8">
    <meta                    name="viewport"
content="width=device-width,      initial-
scale=1.0">
    <title>API Data Fetch</title>
</head>
```

```
<body>
    <h1>User List</h1>
    <ul id="userList"></ul>

    <script src="app.js"></script>
</body>
</html>
```

3. **JavaScript Code** (app.js): In this example, we'll fetch data from the JSONPlaceholder API and display the users' names.

```javascript
async function fetchUsers() {
    const        response        =        await
fetch('https://jsonplaceholder.typicode.c
om/users');
    const users = await response.json();
// Parse JSON from the response
    return users;
}

async function displayUsers() {
    try {
        const users = await fetchUsers();
        const        userListElement        =
document.getElementById("userList");
```

```
        users.forEach(user => {
            let        li        =
document.createElement("li");
                li.textContent = user.name;

userListElement.appendChild(li);
            });
        } catch (error) {
            console.error("Error      fetching
users:", error.message);
        }
    }

    // Call the function to display users
    displayUsers();
```

4. **Explanation**:

   o The `fetchUsers()` function uses `fetch()` to make an HTTP request to the JSONPlaceholder API. It then waits for the response to resolve using `await`, and converts the response into a JavaScript object with `response.json()`.

   o The `displayUsers()` function calls `fetchUsers()` to get the list of users and dynamically creates a list item (`<li>`) for each user's name, which is then appended to the `<ul>` element with the id `userList`.

Output: The webpage will display a list of user names fetched from the API.

Summary

In this chapter, you:

- Learned about **Promises**, which solve the issue of callback hell by allowing you to chain asynchronous operations in a cleaner way.
- Explored **async/await**, a more modern and readable way to handle asynchronous operations in JavaScript, making your code look synchronous while keeping it non-blocking.
- Built a **real-world example** of fetching data from an API using **async/await** to display a list of users, which shows how powerful these concepts are in simplifying asynchronous code.

Mastering Promises and `async/await` will significantly improve your ability to handle asynchronous code in JavaScript, leading to more readable, maintainable, and efficient applications.

CHAPTER 11

JAVASCRIPT EVENTS AND DOM MANIPULATION

Understanding the Document Object Model (DOM)

The **Document Object Model (DOM)** is a programming interface for web documents. It represents the structure of a webpage as a tree of nodes, where each node corresponds to an element, attribute, or piece of text in the document. JavaScript can interact with the DOM to manipulate the content, structure, and style of a webpage dynamically.

1. **What is the DOM?**
    o   The DOM provides a structured representation of the HTML document as a tree. This tree structure allows JavaScript to access, modify, add, and delete elements and content within a webpage.
    o   Each HTML element is represented as a **node** in the DOM tree. For example, a `<div>`, `<p>`, and `<button>` are all nodes.

2. **DOM Structure Example**: Given the following HTML:

```
html
```

```
<div id="container">
    <h1>Welcome to My Website</h1>
    <p>This is a paragraph.</p>
    <button      id="clickMeButton">Click
Me</button>
</div>
```

The DOM structure would look something like this:

```
less
```

```
document
    └── html
        └── body
            └── div#container
                ├── h1
                └── p
                └── button#clickMeButton
```

In the above tree, each element (div, h1, p, button) is a node, and JavaScript can interact with these nodes to modify the page's content and structure.

3. **Accessing DOM Elements**: JavaScript provides several methods for accessing and manipulating elements in the DOM. Some common ones are:

   o **getElementById()**: Returns the element with the specified id.

127

- o **getElementsByClassName()**: Returns a collection of elements with the specified class name.
- o **querySelector()**: Returns the first element that matches the CSS selector.
- o **querySelectorAll()**: Returns all elements that match the CSS selector.

Example:

```javascript
let button =
document.getElementById('clickMeButton');
console.log(button); // Logs the <button>
element to the console
```

4. **Manipulating DOM Elements**: Once an element is accessed, you can modify its content, attributes, and styles:
   - o **Change the content**: element.innerHTML or element.textContent
   - o **Change the styles**: element.style.property = value
   - o **Add/Remove attributes**: element.setAttribute(), element.removeAttribute()

Example:

```javascript
let paragraph = document.querySelector('p');
paragraph.textContent = "This is the new text!"; // Change the text of the <p> element
paragraph.style.color = "blue"; // Change the text color to blue
```

Event Handling and Propagation

Events in JavaScript are actions that occur in response to user interaction or other stimuli, such as clicks, keyboard inputs, or page load events. Understanding **event handling** and **event propagation** is crucial for creating interactive web applications.

1. **Event Handling**: Event handling allows JavaScript to respond to user actions like clicks, mouse movements, key presses, and more. To handle an event, you attach an **event listener** to an HTML element. The event listener listens for a specific event and executes a function when the event occurs.

   o **Syntax**:

   ```javascript
   javascript
   ```

129

```
element.addEventListener('event',
function);
```

- **element**: The HTML element you want to add the event to.
- **'event'**: The type of event (e.g., 'click', 'mouseover', 'keydown').
- **function**: The function to run when the event occurs.

Example:

```
javascript
```

```
let            button            =
document.getElementById('clickMeButton');

button.addEventListener('click',
function() {
    alert("Button was clicked!");
});
```

- o In this example, when the button with the id clickMeButton is clicked, the function will run and show an alert saying "Button was clicked!"

2. **Event Propagation**: Event propagation refers to the way events propagate (or bubble) through the DOM. There are two main phases of event propagation:

- o **Capturing Phase**: The event is captured from the outermost element and passed down the DOM tree to the target element.

- o **Bubbling Phase**: After the event reaches the target element, it bubbles up the DOM tree to the outer elements.

- o By default, events bubble up from the target element to its ancestors, which allows for event delegation (handling events at a higher level in the DOM rather than directly on the target element).

3. **Stopping Event Propagation**: You can stop the event from propagating using `event.stopPropagation()`. This is useful if you want to prevent other event listeners on parent elements from being triggered.

Example:

```javascript

document.getElementById('outerDiv').addEv
entListener('click', function() {
    console.log("Outer div clicked");
});

document.getElementById('innerDiv').addEv
entListener('click', function(event) {
```

```
    event.stopPropagation();  // Stops the
event from bubbling up to the outer div
    console.log("Inner div clicked");
});
```

- o In this example, when the inner div is clicked, the event will not bubble to the outer div because `event.stopPropagation()` is called.

Real-world Example: Making a Button Interactive

Let's create an interactive button that changes the background color of a webpage when clicked. We'll use DOM manipulation and event handling to achieve this.

1. **HTML Structure**: Create a simple HTML page with a button and a paragraph:

```
html
```

```
<!DOCTYPE html>
<html lang="en">
<head>
    <meta charset="UTF-8">
    <meta                name="viewport"
content="width=device-width,      initial-
scale=1.0">
    <title>Interactive Button</title>
```

```
</head>
<body>
    <h1>Click the Button to Change the
Background Color</h1>
    <button    id="changeColorBtn">Change
Color</button>
    <p    id="status">Current    color:
White</p>

    <script src="app.js"></script>
</body>
</html>
```

2. **CSS Styling** (styles.css): Optional, to style the button and text:

css

```
body {
    font-family: Arial, sans-serif;
    text-align: center;
    margin-top: 50px;
}

button {
    padding: 10px 20px;
    font-size: 16px;
    background-color: #4CAF50;
    color: white;
    border: none;
```

133

```
    border-radius: 5px;

    cursor: pointer;

}


button:hover {

    background-color: #45a049;

}


#status {

    margin-top: 20px;

}
```

3. **JavaScript Code** (app.js): Now, let's add interactivity to the button using JavaScript. When the button is clicked, the background color of the webpage will change, and the status paragraph will update to reflect the current color.

```javascript
let              button              =
document.getElementById('changeColorBtn')
;
let              status              =
document.getElementById('status');

button.addEventListener('click',
function() {
    let colors = ['red', 'blue', 'green',
'yellow', 'purple', 'pink'];
```

```
    let          currentColor          =
document.body.style.backgroundColor;

    // Choose a random color from the array
    let          newColor          =
colors[Math.floor(Math.random()          *
colors.length)];

    // Change the background color and
update the status text
    document.body.style.backgroundColor =
newColor;
    status.textContent = `Current color:
${newColor}`;
});
```

Explanation:

- o We access the button (#changeColorBtn) and the paragraph (#status) elements using getElementById.
- o We add an event listener to the button so that when it's clicked, the background color of the page changes to a random color from the colors array.
- o The current background color is displayed in the paragraph (#status) to give the user feedback.

4. **How it Works**:

o When the button is clicked, the event listener triggers the callback function.

o The function selects a random color from the `colors` array using `Math.random()` and applies it to the `backgroundColor` property of the `body` element.

o The status text is updated to reflect the new background color.

Example Output:

```css
css


(After clicking the button)
Current color: blue
```

Summary

In this chapter, you:

- Gained a deeper understanding of the **Document Object Model (DOM)** and how it represents HTML elements as objects that can be manipulated using JavaScript.
- Learned how to handle **events** in JavaScript, including attaching event listeners, using the `addEventListener()` method, and handling event propagation with `stopPropagation()`.

136

- Built a **real-world example** of an interactive button that changes the background color of the page, demonstrating how to use event handling and DOM manipulation together.

Mastering DOM manipulation and event handling is crucial for building interactive and dynamic web applications. These skills allow you to create engaging user interfaces and respond to user actions in real time.

CHAPTER 12

MANIPULATING THE DOM WITH JAVASCRIPT

Selecting and Modifying DOM Elements

In JavaScript, the **DOM (Document Object Model)** allows you to interact with and manipulate HTML elements. By using the appropriate DOM methods, you can select elements, modify their properties, and dynamically update the content of your webpage. Here, we'll go over how to select and modify DOM elements using JavaScript.

1. **Selecting DOM Elements**: There are various ways to select elements in the DOM. The most common methods are:

    o   **getElementById()**: Selects an element by its ID.

    ```javascript
    let element = document.getElementById('myElement');
    ```

- o **getElementsByClassName()**: Selects all elements with a specified class.

```javascript
let elements = document.getElementsByClassName('my Class');
```

- o **getElementsByTagName()**: Selects all elements with a specified tag name.

```javascript
let elements = document.getElementsByTagName('p');
```

- o **querySelector()**: Selects the first element that matches a specified CSS selector.

```javascript
let element = document.querySelector('.myClass');
```

- o **querySelectorAll()**: Selects all elements that match a specified CSS selector.

```javascript
```

```
let            elements        =
document.querySelectorAll('.myClass
');
```

2. **Example**:
3. javascript
4.
5. let   heading   =
   document.querySelector('h1');
6. console.log(heading.textContent); // Logs
   the text content of the first <h1> element
7. **Modifying DOM Elements**: Once you've selected an element, you can modify it using properties like textContent, innerHTML, style, and others.

   o **Changing Text Content**:

   ```
   javascript
   ```

   ```
   let            heading          =
   document.querySelector('h1');
   heading.textContent = "New  Heading
   Text";
   ```

   o **Changing HTML Content**:

   ```
   javascript
   ```

   ```
   let            paragraph        =
   document.querySelector('p');
   ```

```
paragraph.innerHTML = "<strong>This
is bold text!</strong>";
```

o **Changing Styles**: You can directly modify CSS styles of an element through JavaScript.

```
javascript
```

```
let              box            =
document.querySelector('.box');
box.style.backgroundColor = "blue";
box.style.width = "200px";
```

o **Adding/Removing Classes**: JavaScript provides methods to add or remove classes from elements dynamically.

```
javascript
```

```
let             button            =
document.querySelector('button');
button.classList.add('active');   //
Adds the 'active' class
button.classList.remove('active');
// Removes the 'active' class
```

141

Adding and Removing Elements Dynamically

JavaScript allows you to create, add, and remove elements from the DOM dynamically. This capability is essential for building interactive websites where content can change based on user input or other events.

1. **Creating New Elements**: You can create new HTML elements using `document.createElement()` and then append them to the DOM using methods like `appendChild()` or `insertBefore()`.

   Example:

   ```javascript
   // Create a new paragraph element
   let           newParagraph           =
   document.createElement('p');
   newParagraph.textContent  =  "This  is  a
   dynamically created paragraph.";

   // Append the new paragraph to the body
   document.body.appendChild(newParagraph);
   ```

2. **Appending and Prepending Elements**: Once an element is created, it can be added to an existing element using `appendChild()` (to add to the end of a container) or `prepend()` (to add to the beginning).

142

Example:

```
javascript
```

```
let            container            =
document.querySelector('.container');
let            newDiv               =
document.createElement('div');
newDiv.textContent = "This is a new div.";


// Append the new div to the container
container.appendChild(newDiv);
```

3. **Removing Elements**: You can remove elements from the DOM using `removeChild()` or `remove()`. If you want to remove an element that you have selected, you can call the `remove()` method on that element.

Example:

```
javascript
```

```
let            elementToRemove           =
document.querySelector('.removeMe');
elementToRemove.remove();   // Removes the
element from the DOM
```

o   If you want to remove a child element from a parent element, you can use `removeChild()`:

143

```javascript
let                    parent            =
document.querySelector('.parent');
let              child              =
document.querySelector('.child');
parent.removeChild(child);            //
Removes the child from the parent
```

4. **Inserting Elements at Specific Positions**: You can insert new elements at specific positions within the DOM using methods like `insertBefore()` and `insertAdjacentElement()`.

Example:

```javascript
let                parent              =
document.querySelector('#parent');
let              newElement            =
document.createElement('p');
newElement.textContent  =  "New  element
inserted at the beginning.";

parent.insertBefore(newElement,
parent.firstChild);    //  Inserts  at  the
beginning
```

Real-world Example: Building a Dynamic Image Gallery

In this example, we will build a dynamic image gallery that allows users to add new images, remove existing ones, and update image captions. This will involve selecting, modifying, adding, and removing DOM elements.

1. **HTML Structure**: Create an HTML file with a basic layout for the image gallery and controls for adding and removing images.

html

```
<!DOCTYPE html>
<html lang="en">
<head>
    <meta charset="UTF-8">
    <meta                 name="viewport"
content="width=device-width,     initial-
scale=1.0">
    <title>Dynamic Image Gallery</title>
</head>
<body>
    <h1>Dynamic Image Gallery</h1>

    <button          id="addImageBtn">Add
Image</button>
    <div id="gallery">
        <div class="image-item">
```

145

```
            <img          src="image1.jpg"
alt="Image 1">
            <p>Image 1 Caption</p>
            <button
class="removeBtn">Remove</button>
        </div>
        <div class="image-item">
            <img          src="image2.jpg"
alt="Image 2">
            <p>Image 2 Caption</p>
            <button
class="removeBtn">Remove</button>
        </div>
    </div>

    <script src="app.js"></script>
</body>
</html>
```

2. **CSS Styling** (styles.css): Style the gallery with some basic CSS.

css

```
#gallery {
    display: flex;
    gap: 20px;
    flex-wrap: wrap;
}
```

```css
.image-item {
    border: 1px solid #ddd;
    padding: 10px;
    width: 200px;
    text-align: center;
}

img {
    max-width: 100%;
    height: auto;
}

button {
    margin-top: 10px;
    padding: 5px 10px;
    background-color: red;
    color: white;
    border: none;
    cursor: pointer;
}

button:hover {
    background-color: darkred;
}
```

3. **JavaScript Code** (app.js): This script will add functionality to dynamically add and remove images from the gallery.

```javascript
javascript

// Function to add a new image to the
gallery
document.getElementById('addImageBtn').ad
dEventListener('click', function() {
    let            gallery            =
document.getElementById('gallery');
    let           newImageItem         =
document.createElement('div');
    newImageItem.classList.add('image-
item');

    let           newImage             =
document.createElement('img');
    newImage.src = 'newImage.jpg';    //
Replace with your image path
    newImage.alt = 'New Image';

    let           caption              =
document.createElement('p');
    caption.textContent  =  'New   Image
Caption';

    let           removeButton         =
document.createElement('button');

removeButton.classList.add('removeBtn');
    removeButton.textContent = 'Remove';
```

```
    // Append the new image item to the
gallery
    newImageItem.appendChild(newImage);
    newImageItem.appendChild(caption);

newImageItem.appendChild(removeButton);
    gallery.appendChild(newImageItem);

    // Add event listener to the remove
button

removeButton.addEventListener('click',
function() {

gallery.removeChild(newImageItem);
    });
});

// Remove image functionality for existing
images
let          removeButtons           =
document.querySelectorAll('.removeBtn');
removeButtons.forEach(function(button) {
    button.addEventListener('click',
function() {
        let          imageItem          =
button.closest('.image-item');
```

149

```
document.getElementById('gallery').remove
Child(imageItem);
    });
});
```

4. **Explanation**:

   o   When the **"Add Image"** button is clicked, the script creates a new image element and appends it to the gallery. The image is given a default source (`newImage.jpg`), and a caption is added beneath it.

   o   Each image has a **Remove** button that, when clicked, removes the corresponding image item from the gallery.

   o   The remove functionality is implemented by adding an event listener to each **Remove** button, and when clicked, it removes the parent `.image-item` element.

150

Summary

In this chapter, you:

- Learned how to **select and modify DOM elements** using methods like `getElementById()`, `querySelector()`, and others.
- Explored how to **dynamically add and remove elements** using `createElement()`, `appendChild()`, `removeChild()`, and `remove()`.
- Built a **dynamic image gallery** where users can add new images, remove images, and update captions, demonstrating how to interact with the DOM dynamically.

Manipulating the DOM is a key skill for building interactive web pages, and mastering these techniques allows you to create highly dynamic and user-responsive websites.

151

CHAPTER 13

FORM VALIDATION AND USER INPUT

Validating Forms with JavaScript

Form validation is an essential part of any web application. It ensures that the data entered by the user is valid before it is submitted to the server. JavaScript plays a crucial role in performing client-side validation, allowing you to provide immediate feedback to the user.

1. **Why Validate Forms?**

    o **Ensure correct data**: Validation helps ensure that the data entered is in the correct format (e.g., a valid email address or phone number).

    o **Improve user experience**: Instant validation feedback helps users correct errors before submitting the form, reducing the likelihood of submission failures.

    o **Security**: Validating forms on the client side can catch basic errors, but server-side validation is always necessary to prevent malicious data from being processed.

2. **Common Form Validation Scenarios**:

   o   Required fields (e.g., name, email, password)

   o   Email format (e.g., `name@domain.com`)

   o   Number ranges (e.g., age between 18 and 100)

   o   Matching passwords (e.g., confirm password field)

3. **Basic Form Validation in JavaScript**: To perform form validation in JavaScript, you can listen for the form's `submit` event and check if the fields meet the required conditions before allowing the form to submit.

Example:

html

```
<form id="signupForm">
    <label for="email">Email:</label>
    <input    type="email"    id="email"
name="email" required>
    <br><br>
    <label
for="password">Password:</label>
    <input type="password" id="password"
name="password" required>
    <br><br>
    <button type="submit">Submit</button>
</form>
```

153

```
<div   id="errorMessage"   style="color:
red;"></div>

<script>

document.getElementById('signupForm').add
EventListener('submit', function(event) {
        event.preventDefault();         //
Prevent form submission

        let          email          =
document.getElementById('email').value;
        let        password        =
document.getElementById('password').value
;
        let errorMessage = '';

        // Validate email
        if (!email.includes('@')) {
            errorMessage += 'Please enter
a valid email address.<br>';
        }

        // Validate password length
        if (password.length < 6) {
            errorMessage += 'Password must
be at least 6 characters long.<br>';
        }
```

```
        // Show error messages or submit
the form
        if (errorMessage) {

document.getElementById('errorMessage').i
nnerHTML = errorMessage;
        } else {
            alert('Form          submitted
successfully!');
            // form.submit(); // Uncomment
to allow actual form submission
        }
    });
</script>
```

- o In this example, the form is not submitted until both the email and password fields are validated.
- o If the email is invalid or the password is too short, an error message is displayed, and the form is not submitted.

4. **Using HTML5 Validation**: HTML5 introduces built-in validation features, such as the `required`, `pattern`, `minlength`, and `type` attributes, which can be used in conjunction with JavaScript validation to improve user experience.

Example:

```html
html
```

155

```
<form id="signupForm">
    <label for="email">Email:</label>
    <input      type="email"      id="email"
name="email" required>
    <br><br>
    <label
for="password">Password:</label>
    <input  type="password"  id="password"
name="password" minlength="6" required>
    <br><br>
    <button type="submit">Submit</button>
</form>
```

- o In this example, HTML5 validation ensures that the email field is correctly formatted and the password is at least 6 characters long. JavaScript can still be used for custom validation or handling more complex logic.

Handling User Input and Errors

Handling user input involves not just validation but also providing clear feedback when errors occur. Proper error handling ensures that users are guided to correct their input, which improves both usability and accessibility.

1. **Displaying Validation Errors**: After detecting an error in the user input, you can display helpful messages next to the relevant form field, telling the user what went wrong.

   Example:

```javascript
let email =
document.getElementById('email');
let password =
document.getElementById('password');
let emailError =
document.getElementById('emailError');
let passwordError =
document.getElementById('passwordError');

if (!email.value.includes('@')) {
    emailError.textContent = 'Please enter
a valid email address.';
} else {
    emailError.textContent = '';
}

if (password.value.length < 6) {
    passwordError.textContent = 'Password
must be at least 6 characters long.';
} else {
```

```
        passwordError.textContent = '';
}
```

HTML:

```
html

<form id="signupForm">
    <label for="email">Email:</label>
    <input    type="email"    id="email"
name="email" required>
    <div   id="emailError"   style="color:
red;"></div>

    <br><br>

    <label
for="password">Password:</label>
    <input  type="password"  id="password"
name="password" required>
    <div  id="passwordError"  style="color:
red;"></div>

    <br><br>
    <button type="submit">Submit</button>
</form>
```

> o In this example, error messages are displayed
>   next to the fields that have invalid input,
>   improving the user experience.

158

2. **Focus on Error Fields**: You can also make the user experience better by highlighting fields that need attention or focusing on them after the user submits the form with errors.

Example:

javascript

```
if (!email.value.includes('@')) {
    email.focus();   // Focus on the email
field
}
```

3. **Custom Error Handling**: For complex validation logic, you can implement custom error handling. For instance, checking whether the email is unique, or verifying passwords match.

Real-world Example: Creating a Sign-Up Form with Validation

Let's now put everything together by creating a **sign-up form** with basic validation. We'll use JavaScript to validate the form, ensuring the user inputs a valid email address, password, and matching "confirm password" field before submitting the form.

1. **HTML Structure**:

html

```html
<form id="signUpForm">
    <label for="email">Email:</label>
    <input type="email" id="email"
name="email" required>
    <div id="emailError" style="color:
red;"></div>
    <br><br>

    <label
for="password">Password:</label>
    <input type="password" id="password"
name="password" required>
    <div id="passwordError" style="color:
red;"></div>
    <br><br>

    <label for="confirmPassword">Confirm
Password:</label>
    <input type="password"
id="confirmPassword"
name="confirmPassword" required>
    <div id="confirmPasswordError"
style="color: red;"></div>
    <br><br>

    <button type="submit">Sign Up</button>
</form>
```

160

```
<script src="app.js"></script>
```

2. **CSS Styling** (`styles.css`):

css

```css
form {
    max-width: 400px;
    margin: 0 auto;
}

label {
    font-weight: bold;
}

input {
    width: 100%;
    padding: 8px;
    margin: 5px 0;
}

button {
    padding: 10px 20px;
    font-size: 16px;
    background-color: #4CAF50;
    color: white;
    border: none;
    cursor: pointer;
}
```

```css
button:hover {
    background-color: #45a049;
}
```

3. **JavaScript Code** (app.js):

```
javascript
```

```javascript
document.getElementById('signUpForm').add
EventListener('submit', function(event) {
    event.preventDefault();    // Prevent
the form from submitting

    let          email          =
document.getElementById('email').value;
    let          password          =
document.getElementById('password').value
;
    let          confirmPassword          =
document.getElementById('confirmPassword'
).value;

    let          emailError          =
document.getElementById('emailError');
    let          passwordError          =
document.getElementById('passwordError');
    let          confirmPasswordError          =
document.getElementById('confirmPasswordE
rror');
```

162

```javascript
    let isValid = true;

    // Validate email
    if (!email.includes('@')) {
        emailError.textContent  =  'Please
enter a valid email address.';
        isValid = false;
    } else {
        emailError.textContent = '';
    }

    // Validate password
    if (password.length < 6) {
        passwordError.textContent         =
'Password  must  be  at  least  6  characters
long.';
        isValid = false;
    } else {
        passwordError.textContent = '';
    }

    // Validate confirm password
    if (password !== confirmPassword) {
        confirmPasswordError.textContent =
'Passwords do not match.';
        isValid = false;
    } else {
```

```
        confirmPasswordError.textContent =
'';
    }

    // If all validations pass, alert
success
    if (isValid) {
        alert('Sign-up successful!');
    }
});
```

4. **Explanation**:

   o The form collects the user's email, password, and confirm password.

   o JavaScript listens for the form submission and validates the input.

   o If the email, password, or confirm password fields are invalid, corresponding error messages are displayed.

   o If all validations pass, the form shows a success message (`alert()`), and the form is not submitted to the server (this is just for the demonstration purpose).

Summary

In this chapter, you:

- Learned how to **validate forms with JavaScript** to ensure that user input meets specific criteria (e.g., valid email, strong password, matching passwords).
- Explored how to **handle user input and errors**, providing meaningful feedback and improving user experience with error messages and input focus.
- Built a **sign-up form** with validation logic that checks the email format, password strength, and password confirmation before submission.

Form validation is an essential part of building user-friendly, secure web applications. By mastering these techniques, you can create smooth, intuitive forms that guide users and prevent invalid or incomplete submissions.

CHAPTER 14

LOCAL STORAGE AND SESSION STORAGE

Storing Data in the Browser

In modern web development, **local storage** and **session storage** allow web applications to store data directly in the user's browser. These web storage mechanisms offer an efficient way to store small amounts of data, making it easy to persist data between sessions or pages. Both **localStorage** and **sessionStorage** are part of the **Web Storage API** and can be accessed through JavaScript.

1. **What is Web Storage?** Web storage provides two types of storage options:

    o **LocalStorage**: Stores data with no expiration time, meaning the data persists even after the browser is closed and reopened.

    o **SessionStorage**: Stores data for the duration of the page session. Data is only available as long as the browser tab or window is open. Once the tab or window is closed, the data is deleted.

2. **Why Use Web Storage?**

166

o **Persistent data**: Both localStorage and sessionStorage allow data to be saved without requiring a backend or database.

o **Performance**: Storing data on the client-side can reduce server load and improve performance, especially for applications that need to store small amounts of data temporarily.

o **Convenience**: Storing data locally makes it easier to keep track of user preferences, cart items, or settings without requiring server-side interactions.

Differences Between LocalStorage and SessionStorage

Although both localStorage and sessionStorage are used for storing data in the browser, they differ in terms of persistence, scope, and use cases:

Feature	localStorage	sessionStorage
Lifetime	Data persists until explicitly deleted or cleared.	Data is cleared when the browser tab or window is closed.

167

Feature	localStorage	sessionStorage
Scope	Accessible across all tabs and windows of the same origin.	Only accessible within the same tab or window.
Capacity	Typically, 5MB per domain (varies by browser).	Typically, 5MB per domain (varies by browser).
Use Case	Storing long-term data (user preferences, authentication tokens, etc.).	Storing temporary data (session information, form data, etc.).
Storage Key	Can store data for as long as the user keeps the browser open.	Data is only available for the duration of a page session.

Example:

javascript

```
// Storing data in localStorage
localStorage.setItem('user', 'JohnDoe');
let user = localStorage.getItem('user');
console.log(user);  // Output: JohnDoe
```

```
// Storing data in sessionStorage
sessionStorage.setItem('sessionId', '12345');
let                    sessionId                    =
sessionStorage.getItem('sessionId');
console.log(sessionId);  // Output: 12345
```

Real-world Example: Building a Simple Notes App

Let's create a simple **Notes App** where users can add and remove notes, and these notes will be stored in the browser using **localStorage**. The app will allow users to persist their notes even after they close the browser.

1. **HTML Structure**: We will create a simple form to add notes and display them in a list. We'll also add a button to delete individual notes.

   html

```
<!DOCTYPE html>
<html lang="en">
<head>
    <meta charset="UTF-8">
    <meta                    name="viewport"
content="width=device-width,        initial-
scale=1.0">
    <title>Notes App</title>
    <style>
```

169

```css
body {
    font-family:    Arial,    sans-serif;
    margin: 20px;
}
input, button {
    padding: 10px;
    font-size: 16px;
}
ul {
    list-style-type: none;
    padding: 0;
}
li {
    background-color: #f4f4f4;
    padding: 10px;
    margin: 5px 0;
    display: flex;
    justify-content:        space-between;
}
button {
    background-color: red;
    color: white;
    border: none;
    cursor: pointer;
}
button:hover {
    background-color: darkred;
```

```
        }
    </style>
</head>
<body>
    <h1>Notes App</h1>
    <input    type="text"    id="noteInput"
placeholder="Enter a new note">
    <button          id="addNoteBtn">Add
Note</button>
    <ul id="notesList"></ul>

    <script src="app.js"></script>
</body>
</html>
```

2. **JavaScript Code** (`app.js`): Now we will use **localStorage** to store the notes so that they persist even after the user closes the browser. When the page is reloaded, the notes will be displayed again.

javascript

```
// Get elements from the DOM
const          noteInput          =
document.getElementById('noteInput');
const          addNoteBtn          =
document.getElementById('addNoteBtn');
const          notesList          =
document.getElementById('notesList');
```

171

```javascript
// Load existing notes from localStorage
const loadNotes = () => {
    const                notes              =
JSON.parse(localStorage.getItem('notes'))
|| [];
    notesList.innerHTML = '';
    notes.forEach((note, index) => {
        const               li            =
document.createElement('li');
        li.innerHTML = `
            ${note}
            <button
onclick="removeNote(${index})">Delete</bu
tton>
        `;
        notesList.appendChild(li);
    });
};

// Add new note
addNoteBtn.addEventListener('click', () =>
{
    const              newNote             =
noteInput.value.trim();
    if (newNote) {
        let               notes            =
JSON.parse(localStorage.getItem('notes'))
|| [];
```

```javascript
        notes.push(newNote);
        localStorage.setItem('notes',
JSON.stringify(notes));
        noteInput.value = '';  // Clear the
input field
        loadNotes();  // Re-load the notes
list
    }
});


// Remove a note
const removeNote = (index) => {
    let              notes               =
JSON.parse(localStorage.getItem('notes'))
|| [];
    notes.splice(index, 1);
    localStorage.setItem('notes',
JSON.stringify(notes));
    loadNotes();  // Re-load the notes list
after removing a note
};


// Initial load of notes when the page is
opened
loadNotes();
```

3. **Explanation**:

    o   **Adding Notes**: When the user types a note and clicks the "Add Note" button, the note is saved to

173

localStorage. We use JSON.stringify() to store the array of notes as a string, since localStorage only supports strings. After adding the note, we call the loadNotes() function to display the notes.

- o **Removing Notes**: When the "Delete" button next to a note is clicked, the removeNote() function is called. It removes the note from the notes array and updates localStorage.

- o **Displaying Notes**: On page load, the loadNotes() function retrieves the notes from localStorage using JSON.parse() and displays them in the list.

4. **How It Works**:

- o As users add and remove notes, the data is updated in localStorage.

- o When the page is reloaded, the loadNotes() function is called to fetch and display the stored notes, providing a persistent experience across page reloads.

174

Summary

In this chapter, you:

- Learned about **localStorage** and **sessionStorage**, their differences, and their use cases for storing data on the client-side.
- Explored how to **store and retrieve data in the browser**, making web applications more efficient and reducing the need for frequent server calls.
- Built a **real-world example** of a **dynamic notes app** that uses **localStorage** to store, retrieve, and remove notes, making the app persist across page reloads.

By mastering localStorage and sessionStorage, you can create more efficient web applications with persistent data storage, improving the user experience and reducing server-side overhead.

CHAPTER 15

JAVASCRIPT ANIMATIONS AND TRANSITIONS

Creating Smooth Animations with JavaScript

JavaScript provides a wide range of methods for creating smooth, interactive animations on web pages. Animations help make websites more engaging and dynamic, enhancing user experience. By manipulating CSS properties directly or using the `requestAnimationFrame()` method, JavaScript allows for smooth animations that can run in sync with the browser's refresh rate.

1. **Basic Animation Using `setInterval()` and `setTimeout()`**: You can create simple animations using `setInterval()` or `setTimeout()`. While `setInterval()` calls a function repeatedly at specified intervals, `setTimeout()` executes a function once after a specified delay.

   However, these methods are generally not ideal for smooth, frame-by-frame animations. For smoother animations, we use `requestAnimationFrame()`, which is optimized for performance and synchronized with the browser's refresh rate.

2. **Using `requestAnimationFrame()` for Smooth Animations**: The `requestAnimationFrame()` method is the preferred way to create smooth animations. It requests that the browser call a specified function to update an animation before the next repaint. This ensures that the animation runs smoothly without unnecessary frame skips.

Syntax:

```javascript

function animate() {
    // Update the animation state
    requestAnimationFrame(animate);    // Recursively call animate() for continuous animation
}


requestAnimationFrame(animate);   // Start the animation
```

Example: Moving a box across the screen

```javascript
```

177

```
let box = document.getElementById('box');
let position = 0;

function moveBox() {
    position += 1;    // Increase the
position value
    box.style.left = position + 'px';   //
Move the box to the right

    if (position < 500) {   // Stop the
animation after 500px
        requestAnimationFrame(moveBox);
// Continue the animation
    }
}

moveBox();  // Start the animation
```

- o The **moveBox()** function continuously updates the box's position and re-renders it using requestAnimationFrame(). The animation stops once the box reaches a position of 500px.

3. **Animating Multiple Properties**: You can animate multiple properties at the same time, such as position, size, color, and opacity, by modifying their values within the animation function.

Example: Moving and changing the color of the box

```javascript
javascript

let box = document.getElementById('box');
let position = 0;

function animateBox() {
    position += 2;  // Move 2px each time
    box.style.left = position + 'px';   //
Move the box to the right
    box.style.backgroundColor            =
`rgb(${position % 255}, 100, 150)`;   //
Change color dynamically

    if (position < 500) {

requestAnimationFrame(animateBox);
    }
}

animateBox();
```

- o Here, the box moves to the right while its background color changes based on the position value.

179

Introduction to CSS Animations with JavaScript Control

While JavaScript provides powerful control over animations, **CSS animations** can be used in conjunction with JavaScript to make animations easier to manage and more declarative. You can trigger, pause, or manipulate CSS animations with JavaScript to create more complex effects and interactions.

1. **Creating CSS Animations**: CSS animations allow you to animate properties of elements, such as colors, sizes, positions, and more. You define keyframes, which specify the start and end states of the animation, and use CSS properties like `animation` to apply the animation to elements.

   CSS Example:

```css
css


@keyframes slide {
    0% {
        left: 0;
    }
    100% {
        left: 500px;
    }
}


.box {
```

```
position: absolute;
width: 50px;
height: 50px;
background-color: red;
animation: slide 2s linear infinite;
}
```

- o This CSS snippet defines an animation called slide that moves a box from left: 0px to left: 500px. The animation lasts 2 seconds and repeats infinitely.

2. **JavaScript Control Over CSS Animations**: JavaScript can be used to start, pause, and control CSS animations dynamically. You can trigger CSS animations by adding or removing CSS classes or manipulating CSS properties directly.

Example: Controlling a CSS animation with JavaScript

```javascript
let box = document.querySelector('.box');

// Start animation by adding a class
document.getElementById('startBtn').addEv
entListener('click', function() {
    box.classList.add('animate');
});
```

```
// Pause animation by removing the class
document.getElementById('pauseBtn').addEv
entListener('click', function() {
    box.classList.remove('animate');
});
```

CSS:

```
css


.animate {
    animation: slide 2s linear infinite;
}
```

o   Here, the animation starts when the "Start" button
     is clicked by adding the `animate` class to the
     box. It pauses when the "Pause" button is clicked
     by removing the `animate` class.

Real-world Example: Animating Elements on Scroll

In this example, we'll create a scroll-based animation where
elements animate into view as the user scrolls down the page. This
kind of effect is commonly used to make websites more
interactive and engaging.

182

1. **HTML Structure**: We will create a page with several elements that animate when they come into the viewport as the user scrolls.

html

```
<div class="content">
    <h1>Scroll to see the animation</h1>
    <div    class="box"    style="height:
400px;">Box 1</div>
    <div    class="box"    style="height:
400px;">Box 2</div>
    <div    class="box"    style="height:
400px;">Box 3</div>
</div>
```

2. **CSS Styling** (styles.css): We will initially set the boxes to be invisible and then fade them in when they come into view during scrolling.

css

```
.box {
    opacity: 0;
    transition: opacity 1s ease-in-out;
    background-color: #3498db;
    color: white;
    text-align: center;
}
```

183

```
.visible {
    opacity: 1;
}

.content {
    margin: 50px auto;
    width: 80%;
}
```

3. **JavaScript Code** (app.js): Using JavaScript, we can listen for the scroll event and add a class (visible) to elements when they enter the viewport.

```
javascript

// Function to check if an element is in
the viewport
function isElementInViewport(el) {
    let rect = el.getBoundingClientRect();
    return rect.top >= 0 && rect.bottom <=
window.innerHeight;
}

// Select all boxes
const             boxes             =
document.querySelectorAll('.box');

// Check for elements on scroll
```

```javascript
window.addEventListener('scroll',
function() {
    boxes.forEach(box => {
        if (isElementInViewport(box)) {
            box.classList.add('visible');
        }
    });
});
```

4. **Explanation**:

   o **CSS**: The boxes start with `opacity: 0`, meaning they are invisible. When the `visible` class is added, their opacity transitions to `1`, making them fade in.

   o **JavaScript**: The `isElementInViewport()` function checks whether an element is within the visible area of the browser window. The scroll event listener checks each box to see if it is in the viewport. If it is, the `visible` class is added, triggering the CSS transition.

5. **How It Works**:

   o As you scroll down the page, the JavaScript checks whether each `.box` element has entered the viewport.

   o Once an element enters the viewport, it becomes visible by adding the `visible` class, which triggers the opacity transition defined in CSS.

Summary

In this chapter, you:

- Learned how to create **smooth animations** using JavaScript and the `requestAnimationFrame()` method, providing high-performance animations.
- Explored **CSS animations** and how JavaScript can control them, allowing for more flexible and declarative animation handling.
- Built a **scroll-based animation** where elements fade into view as the user scrolls down the page, making the webpage more interactive and dynamic.

By combining JavaScript with CSS animations and transitions, you can create engaging, dynamic web experiences that enhance user interaction and create visually appealing effects.

CHAPTER 16

INTEGRATING THIRD-PARTY LIBRARIES

Introduction to Popular Libraries (jQuery, Moment.js, etc.)

Third-party libraries are pre-written JavaScript code that you can integrate into your own projects to save time and avoid reinventing the wheel. These libraries are often created by experienced developers to handle common tasks and functionalities that would otherwise take a significant amount of time to implement.

1. **Why Use Third-Party Libraries?**

   o **Time-saving**: Third-party libraries provide ready-to-use solutions for common tasks like handling DOM manipulation, animations, HTTP requests, and date formatting.

   o **Cross-browser compatibility**: Libraries often handle browser quirks and ensure consistent behavior across different browsers.

   o **Efficiency**: Libraries optimize code and performance, allowing you to focus on the unique aspects of your application rather than dealing with low-level implementation details.

o **Community support**: Popular libraries have large communities that contribute to ongoing maintenance, updates, and troubleshooting.

2. **Popular JavaScript Libraries**:

o **jQuery**: A fast, small, and feature-rich JavaScript library that simplifies DOM manipulation, event handling, and AJAX requests.

o **Moment.js**: A library for parsing, validating, manipulating, and formatting dates and times in JavaScript.

o **Lodash**: A utility library offering a wide range of functions to simplify tasks like working with arrays, objects, and other data structures.

o **Axios**: A promise-based HTTP client for making requests to external APIs.

o **Chart.js**: A simple yet flexible JavaScript library for creating charts and graphs.

o **GSAP (GreenSock Animation Platform)**: A powerful library for creating high-performance animations.

How to Include and Use External Libraries

Including third-party libraries into your project is simple. There are two main ways to do this: using a **CDN** (Content Delivery Network) or downloading and hosting the library locally.

1. **Using a CDN**: A CDN is a network of servers that delivers content to users based on their geographic location. By including a link to a CDN in your HTML file, you can quickly add external libraries to your project without the need to download or host the library yourself.

   Example: Including jQuery via CDN

   ```html
   html

   <script
   src="https://code.jquery.com/jquery-
   3.6.0.min.js"></script>
   ```

   o Simply add the `<script>` tag to your HTML file, and the library will be available to use.
   o Other popular libraries, such as Moment.js, also provide CDN links for easy inclusion.

2. **Downloading and Hosting Libraries Locally**: If you prefer to keep the library files in your project directory, you can download the library from its official website or

repository and then include it in your HTML using the `<script>` tag.

Example: Downloading and linking jQuery locally:

html

```
<script                              src="js/jquery-
3.6.0.min.js"></script>
```

3. **Using npm (Node Package Manager)**: If you're working with a Node.js project or using a build tool like Webpack or Babel, you can install libraries using npm or yarn.

    Example: Install jQuery using npm:

    bash

    ```
    npm install jquery
    ```

    After installation, you can import the library into your JavaScript file:

    javascript

    ```
    import $ from 'jquery';
    ```

190

Real-world Example: Using jQuery to Handle DOM Events

jQuery is one of the most widely used libraries for simplifying DOM manipulation and handling events. It provides an easy-to-use syntax for selecting elements and responding to user interactions such as clicks, key presses, and hover actions.

In this example, we will create a simple interactive webpage that changes the background color of a `div` when it is clicked, and displays a message when the mouse hovers over a button.

1. **HTML Structure**: We'll create a `div` that can be clicked to change its background color and a `button` that triggers a hover effect.

   html

```html
<!DOCTYPE html>
<html lang="en">
<head>
    <meta charset="UTF-8">
    <meta                     name="viewport"
content="width=device-width,      initial-
scale=1.0">
    <title>jQuery      Event      Handling
Example</title>
    <style>
        #colorBox {
            width: 200px;
```

```
            height: 200px;
            background-color: lightblue;
            margin: 20px;
            text-align: center;
            line-height: 200px;
            font-size: 20px;
            border-radius: 10px;
        }

        button {
            padding: 10px 20px;
            font-size: 16px;
            cursor: pointer;
        }
    </style>
</head>
<body>
    <div id="colorBox">Click Me!</div>
    <button id="hoverButton">Hover over
me!</button>

    <script
src="https://code.jquery.com/jquery-
3.6.0.min.js"></script>
    <script src="app.js"></script>
</body>
</html>
```

2. **jQuery Code** (app.js): We will use jQuery to handle the click and hover events for the elements.

```javascript
// Handle click event on the div to change
its background color
$('#colorBox').click(function() {
    $(this).css('background-color',
'lightgreen');
    $(this).text('You clicked me!');
});

// Handle hover event on the button to
change its text
$('#hoverButton').hover(
    function() {
        $(this).text('Mouse is over me!');
    },
    function() {
        $(this).text('Hover over me!');
    }
);
```

3. **Explanation**:

   o **Click Event**: The $('#colorBox').click() function listens for a click on the div with the ID colorBox. When the div is clicked, the background color changes to lightgreen, and

193

the text inside the `div` updates to "You clicked me!".

o **Hover Event**: The `$('#hoverButton').hover()` function listens for mouse hover events on the button with the ID `hoverButton`. The first function inside `hover()` runs when the mouse enters the button area, changing the text to "Mouse is over me!". The second function runs when the mouse leaves the button, restoring the text to "Hover over me!".

Summary

In this chapter, you:

- Learned about **third-party libraries** like **jQuery**, **Moment.js**, and others that help streamline common tasks like DOM manipulation, date handling, and animations.
- Explored how to **include and use external libraries** via CDNs, downloading locally, or using npm for modern JavaScript projects.
- Created a **real-world example** where jQuery is used to handle DOM events, such as clicks and mouse hover, to make a webpage more interactive and dynamic.

Integrating third-party libraries into your project can greatly reduce development time and improve code quality. By using well-established libraries like jQuery, you can easily handle common tasks like DOM manipulation, event handling, and animations while keeping your code clean and efficient.

CHAPTER 17

OBJECT-ORIENTED JAVASCRIPT (OOP)

Classes and Objects in JavaScript

Object-Oriented Programming (OOP) is a programming paradigm that uses "objects" to represent data and methods to operate on that data. JavaScript is a **multi-paradigm** language, meaning it supports both functional programming and object-oriented programming. OOP allows for more modular, reusable, and organized code, especially for large-scale applications.

1. **Objects in JavaScript**: An object is a collection of related data and methods. In JavaScript, objects can hold properties (data) and methods (functions). You can create an object using curly braces {} and separate key-value pairs with a colon.

   Example:

   ```javascript
   let person = {
       name: 'Alice',
   ```

196

```
    age: 25,
    greet: function() {
        console.log(`Hello,    my    name    is
$ {this.name}.`);
    }
};

console.log(person.name);       // Output:
Alice
person.greet(); // Output: Hello, my name
is Alice.
```

2. **Classes in JavaScript**: A **class** is a blueprint for creating objects. It defines properties and methods that objects created from the class will have. Classes were introduced in ES6, making it easier to work with OOP concepts in JavaScript.

Class Syntax:

```javascript

class Person {
    constructor(name, age) {
        this.name = name;
        this.age = age;
    }

    greet() {
```

```
        console.log(`Hello,   my   name   is
${this.name}.`);
    }
}


let person1 = new Person('Alice', 25);
person1.greet();  // Output: Hello, my name
is Alice.
```

- o The **constructor()** method is a special method that is called when a new object is created from a class. It initializes the properties of the object.
- o The **greet()** method is a regular method that objects of the class can call.

Encapsulation, Inheritance, and Polymorphism

These are the three fundamental principles of Object-Oriented Programming.

1. **Encapsulation**: Encapsulation refers to bundling the data (properties) and the methods that operate on the data into a single unit, called a class. It also hides the internal workings of an object, providing a public interface for interacting with the object.

o **Private vs. Public Properties**: JavaScript does not have traditional access modifiers like other languages (e.g., `private`, `protected`). However, you can simulate encapsulation by using closures or **getter** and **setter** methods to control access to private data.

Example:

javascript

```
class BankAccount {
    #balance = 0;  // Private property (not
accessible from outside)

    constructor(owner, balance) {
        this.owner = owner;
        this.#balance = balance;
    }

    // Public method to access private
balance
    getBalance() {
        return this.#balance;
    }

    deposit(amount) {
        if (amount > 0) {
            this.#balance += amount;
```

199

```
        }
    }

    withdraw(amount) {
        if (amount > 0 && this.#balance >=
amount) {
            this.#balance -= amount;
        }
    }
}

let account = new BankAccount('John Doe',
1000);
account.deposit(500);
console.log(account.getBalance());     //
Output: 1500
```

- o In this example, the #balance is a private field, only accessible through the public methods getBalance(), deposit(), and withdraw().

2. **Inheritance**: Inheritance allows one class (child) to inherit properties and methods from another class (parent). This helps reduce code duplication and enhances reusability.

Example:

```
javascript
```

200

```
class Animal {
    constructor(name) {
        this.name = name;
    }

    speak() {
        console.log(`${this.name} makes a
sound.`);
    }
}

class Dog extends Animal {
    constructor(name, breed) {
        super(name);   // Call the parent
class constructor
        this.breed = breed;
    }

    speak() {
        console.log(`${this.name}
barks.`);
    }
}

let dog = new Dog('Rex', 'Golden
Retriever');
dog.speak();  // Output: Rex barks.
```

o The `Dog` class inherits the `name` property and `speak()` method from the `Animal` class. However, the `Dog` class can override the `speak()` method to provide its own implementation.

3. **Polymorphism**: Polymorphism allows different objects to respond to the same method in different ways. It can be achieved through method overriding (as in the inheritance example above) or method overloading (although JavaScript doesn't support overloading in the traditional sense).

Example:

javascript

```
class Cat extends Animal {
    speak() {
        console.log(`${this.name}
meows.`);
    }
}


let cat = new Cat('Whiskers');
cat.speak();  // Output: Whiskers meows.


let dog = new Dog('Rex', 'Labrador');
dog.speak();  // Output: Rex barks.
```

o Both the `Dog` and `Cat` classes override the `speak()` method, but the behavior is different for each class, demonstrating polymorphism.

Real-world Example: Creating a Simple Bank Account System

Let's build a **Bank Account System** using OOP principles. We will create a `BankAccount` class to manage account balance and a `Transaction` class for deposits and withdrawals. We'll use **encapsulation** to protect the balance and **inheritance** to extend the functionality with different types of accounts.

1. **HTML Structure**: Let's define the structure for our simple interface (though this is a basic example and won't involve a UI for interaction).

html

```html
<h1>Bank Account System</h1>
<p id="accountInfo"></p>
<button onclick="depositMoney()">Deposit $500</button>
<button onclick="withdrawMoney()">Withdraw $200</button>

<script src="app.js"></script>
```

203

2. **JavaScript Code** (app.js):

```javascript
class BankAccount {
    #balance = 0;  // Private balance

    constructor(owner, balance) {
        this.owner = owner;
        this.#balance = balance;
    }

    // Encapsulation: public method to
access private balance
    getBalance() {
        return this.#balance;
    }

    deposit(amount) {
        if (amount > 0) {
            this.#balance += amount;
        }
    }

    withdraw(amount) {
        if (amount > 0 && this.#balance >=
amount) {
            this.#balance -= amount;
        }
    }
```

204

```javascript
    displayInfo() {
        return `${this.owner}'s  balance:
$$${this.getBalance()}`;
    }
}


// Inherit from BankAccount to create
different types of accounts
class SavingsAccount extends BankAccount {
    constructor(owner, balance) {
        super(owner, balance);
        this.interestRate = 0.05;  // 5%
interest
    }

    // Polymorphism: Overriding deposit
method to include interest
    deposit(amount) {
        super.deposit(amount);
        const interest = amount *
this.interestRate;
        super.deposit(interest);  // Add
interest to balance
    }
}

let myAccount = new SavingsAccount('John
Doe', 1000);
```

205

```
document.getElementById('accountInfo').in
nerHTML = myAccount.displayInfo();

function depositMoney() {
    myAccount.deposit(500);

document.getElementById('accountInfo').in
nerHTML = myAccount.displayInfo();
}

function withdrawMoney() {
    myAccount.withdraw(200);

document.getElementById('accountInfo').in
nerHTML = myAccount.displayInfo();
}
```

3. **Explanation**:

   o **BankAccount Class**: Encapsulates the balance and provides methods for depositing, withdrawing, and displaying account info. The balance is stored as a private property (#balance).

   o **SavingsAccount Class**: Inherits from BankAccount and overrides the deposit() method to add interest to the deposit. This demonstrates **inheritance** and **polymorphism**.

206

- o **User Interaction**: Users can interact with the bank account by depositing or withdrawing money. The balance is updated and displayed after each transaction.

Summary

In this chapter, you:

- Explored **Object-Oriented JavaScript (OOP)** concepts, including **classes**, **objects**, **encapsulation**, **inheritance**, and **polymorphism**.
- Learned how to use **classes** and **constructors** to create reusable templates for objects and how to manage private data using encapsulation.
- Built a **real-world example** of a **bank account system** that utilizes OOP principles to manage transactions and balances with additional functionality like interest accrual in savings accounts.

Mastering **OOP** in JavaScript allows you to build more organized, maintainable, and scalable code, especially for large applications that require complex logic and data management.

CHAPTER 18

JAVASCRIPT DESIGN PATTERNS

Introduction to Design Patterns in JavaScript

A **design pattern** is a reusable solution to a common problem in software design. Design patterns are not code snippets, but rather templates or blueprints that can be adapted to specific situations. They provide a structured way to solve problems and are essential for writing maintainable, scalable, and organized code.

In JavaScript, design patterns are particularly useful when building large applications, especially in complex scenarios involving object creation, event handling, or managing state. They help avoid reinventing the wheel and ensure consistency across the codebase.

Why Use Design Patterns?

- **Reusability**: Design patterns provide solutions that can be reused across different parts of the application.
- **Scalability**: Patterns help ensure that the application structure can scale as it grows.
- **Maintainability**: A standardized approach to solving problems makes code easier to maintain and extend.

Common Patterns: Singleton, Factory, Observer

1. **Singleton Pattern**: The **Singleton** pattern ensures that a class has only one instance and provides a global point of access to that instance. It is used when you need to ensure that only one object is created, for example, in cases like managing configuration or database connections.

   Implementation:

   o A Singleton object is created once, and any subsequent requests for the object return the same instance.

   Example:

   ```javascript
   javascript

   class AppConfig {
       constructor() {
           if (AppConfig.instance) {
               return AppConfig.instance;  // Return the same instance if it exists
           }
           this.config = { theme: 'dark', language: 'en' };
           AppConfig.instance = this; // Save the instance for future access
   ```

209

```
    }

    getConfig() {
        return this.config;
    }

    setConfig(newConfig) {
        this.config = newConfig;
    }
}

const config1 = new AppConfig();
const config2 = new AppConfig();

console.log(config1 === config2);   //
Output: true, both are the same instance
```

- o **Explanation**: The `AppConfig` class ensures that only one instance is created. If you try to create a new instance, the same instance is returned, ensuring the Singleton behavior.

2. **Factory Pattern**: The **Factory** pattern provides an interface for creating objects without specifying the exact class of object that will be created. It is useful when you need to create different types of objects based on certain conditions.

Example:

210

```javascript
javascript

class Car {
    constructor(model) {
        this.model = model;
    }
    drive() {
        console.log(`${this.model}        is
driving!`);
    }
}

class Bike {
    constructor(model) {
        this.model = model;
    }
    ride() {
        console.log(`${this.model}        is
riding!`);
    }
}

class VehicleFactory {
    static createVehicle(type, model) {
        if (type === 'car') {
            return new Car(model);
        } else if (type === 'bike') {
            return new Bike(model);
        } else {
```

```
        throw new Error('Vehicle type
not supported');
        }
    }
}


const            myCar            =
VehicleFactory.createVehicle('car',
'Toyota');
const            myBike           =
VehicleFactory.createVehicle('bike',
'Yamaha');


myCar.drive();    // Output: Toyota is
driving!
myBike.ride();    // Output: Yamaha is
riding!
```

- o **Explanation**: The `VehicleFactory` creates either a `Car` or a `Bike` object based on the specified type, abstracting the object creation process and allowing for future extensions.

3. **Observer Pattern**: The **Observer** pattern defines a one-to-many dependency between objects, where a change in one object triggers updates in other dependent objects. It is useful when you need to notify multiple parts of the application when a change occurs, like in event-driven systems or state management.

Example:

```javascript

class Subject {
    constructor() {
        this.observers = [];
    }

    addObserver(observer) {
        this.observers.push(observer);
    }

    removeObserver(observer) {
        const             index             =
this.observers.indexOf(observer);
        if (index > -1) {
            this.observers.splice(index,
1);
        }
    }

    notifyObservers(message) {
        this.observers.forEach(observer =>
observer.update(message));
    }
}

class Observer {
    constructor(name) {
```

213

```
        this.name = name;
    }

    update(message) {
        console.log(`${this.name}
received: ${message}`);
    }
}

const subject = new Subject();
const observer1 = new Observer('Observer
1');
const observer2 = new Observer('Observer
2');

subject.addObserver(observer1);
subject.addObserver(observer2);

subject.notifyObservers('New        update
available!');

// Output:
// Observer 1 received: New update
available!
// Observer 2 received: New update
available!
```

- o **Explanation**: The Subject class manages a list
  of observers and notifies them when a change

214

occurs. The `Observer` class listens for notifications and updates its state accordingly.

Real-world Example: Implementing a Singleton for App Configuration

In this real-world example, we'll implement a **Singleton** pattern for managing the configuration of an application. The configuration settings, such as theme and language, should remain consistent across different parts of the application and should only be instantiated once.

1. **HTML Structure**: We'll create a simple interface where users can change the application's theme and language settings.

   html

   ```html
   <h1>App Configuration</h1>
   <div>
       <label              for="theme">Select
   Theme:</label>
       <select id="theme">
           <option
   value="light">Light</option>
           <option value="dark">Dark</option>
       </select>
   ```

```
</div>

<div>
    <label          for="language">Select
Language:</label>
    <select id="language">
        <option
value="en">English</option>
        <option
value="es">Spanish</option>
    </select>
</div>

<div>
    <button   onclick="showConfig()">Show
Current Config</button>
</div>

<p id="configOutput"></p>

<script src="app.js"></script>
```

2. **JavaScript Code** (app.js): We'll create a Singleton AppConfig class to manage theme and language settings. Users will be able to change the settings, and the Singleton will ensure that the configuration is consistent across the application.

```
javascript
```

```
class AppConfig {
    // Private static variable to hold the
instance
    static instance;

    constructor() {
        if (AppConfig.instance) {
            return AppConfig.instance;  //
Return the same instance
        }
        this.config = {
            theme: 'light',   // Default
theme
            language: 'en'    // Default
language
        };
        AppConfig.instance = this;  // Save
the instance
    }

    getConfig() {
        return this.config;
    }

    setConfig(newConfig) {
        this.config = { ...this.config,
...newConfig };
    }
```

217

```
}

// Create  a  new  instance  (Singleton
behavior)
const appConfig = new AppConfig();

// Handle theme and language changes
document.getElementById('theme').addEvent
Listener('change', function() {
    appConfig.setConfig({            theme:
this.value });
});

document.getElementById('language').addEv
entListener('change', function() {
    appConfig.setConfig({         language:
this.value });
});

// Show current configuration
function showConfig() {
    const config = appConfig.getConfig();

document.getElementById('configOutput').t
extContent  =  `Theme:  ${config.theme},
Language: ${config.language}`;
}
```

3. **Explanation**:

o **Singleton**: The `AppConfig` class ensures that only one instance of the configuration is created. If the `AppConfig` constructor is called again, the same instance is returned.

o **Managing Configuration**: Users can change the theme and language via `<select>` elements. The `AppConfig` instance updates the configuration accordingly.

o **Show Configuration**: The `showConfig()` function displays the current configuration when the user clicks the "Show Current Config" button.

Summary

In this chapter, you:

- Explored **JavaScript Design Patterns**, including the **Singleton**, **Factory**, and **Observer** patterns.
- Learned how to implement a **Singleton** pattern to ensure a single point of access for shared resources (such as application configuration).
- Built a **real-world example** of a simple **Singleton-based App Configuration** system, where users can modify global settings (like theme and language) with a single shared configuration instance.

Design patterns provide powerful solutions to common problems, and by integrating them into your JavaScript code, you can create more efficient, maintainable, and scalable applications. Understanding and applying design patterns is essential for professional-level development, especially in large or complex applications.

CHAPTER 19

FUNCTIONAL PROGRAMMING IN JAVASCRIPT

Understanding Functional Programming Concepts

Functional Programming (FP) is a programming paradigm that treats computation as the evaluation of mathematical functions and avoids changing state or mutable data. In contrast to **imperative programming**, which focuses on changing state and step-by-step execution, FP emphasizes the use of functions to transform data.

In JavaScript, functional programming concepts are particularly useful for writing clean, readable, and maintainable code. The main principles of functional programming are:

1. **Immutability**: Data is never modified directly; instead, new data structures are created based on transformations.
2. **First-class Functions**: Functions are treated as first-class citizens, meaning they can be passed as arguments, returned from other functions, and assigned to variables.

3. **Pure Functions**: A pure function is one that always produces the same output for the same input and has no side effects (i.e., it doesn't modify any external state).

4. **Function Composition**: The process of combining multiple functions to create a new function that performs a more complex task.

5. **Declarative Code**: Instead of focusing on how to perform an operation, functional programming focuses on what to do (i.e., the logic or transformation).

Higher-order Functions, Currying, and Composition

1. **Higher-order Functions**: A **higher-order function** is a function that takes one or more functions as arguments, returns a function as a result, or both. In JavaScript, functions are first-class citizens, so they can be passed around as arguments or returned from other functions.

Example:

```
javascript

function add(a, b) {
    return a + b;
}

function calculate(fn, a, b) {
```

```
    return  fn(a,  b);    // Higher-order
function
}

console.log(calculate(add,  5,  3));    //
Output: 8
```

- o **Explanation**: The `calculate` function is a higher-order function because it takes another function (`add`) as an argument and calls it with `a` and `b`.

2. **Currying**: **Currying** is the process of breaking down a function that takes multiple arguments into a series of functions that each take one argument. Currying allows you to create specialized functions by fixing some arguments.

Example:

```javascript

function multiply(a) {
    return function(b) {
        return a * b;
    };
}

const multiplyBy2 = multiply(2);
```

223

```
console.log(multiplyBy2(5));    // Output:
10
```

- o **Explanation**: The `multiply` function returns another function that takes the second argument b. The `multiplyBy2` function is a partially applied function that multiplies any given number by 2.

3. **Function Composition**: **Function composition** is the process of combining two or more functions to create a new function. The output of one function is passed as the input to the next.

Example:

```
javascript

function add5(x) {
    return x + 5;
}

function multiplyBy3(x) {
    return x * 3;
}

function compose(f, g) {
    return function(x) {
        return f(g(x));
    };
```

```
}
```

```
const         add5ThenMultiplyBy3      =
compose(multiplyBy3, add5);
console.log(add5ThenMultiplyBy3(2));    //
Output: 21
```

- o **Explanation**: The `compose` function takes two functions `f` and `g`, and returns a new function that applies `g` first, then `f` to the result. Here, `add5ThenMultiplyBy3` first adds 5 to the input and then multiplies the result by 3.

Real-world Example: Building a Functional Calculator

Let's apply the functional programming concepts to create a **simple calculator**. We will create an object that contains basic arithmetic functions like add, subtract, multiply, and divide. We will demonstrate **higher-order functions**, **currying**, and **function composition** in the implementation.

1. **HTML Structure**: Let's create a simple interface for the calculator with buttons for numbers and operations.

```html
<h1>Functional Calculator</h1>
```

```html
<input type="text" id="display" readonly>
<div>
    <button
onclick="pressNumber(1)">1</button>
    <button
onclick="pressNumber(2)">2</button>
    <button
onclick="pressNumber(3)">3</button>
    <button
onclick="pressOperator('+')">+</button>
</div>
<div>
    <button
onclick="pressNumber(4)">4</button>
    <button
onclick="pressNumber(5)">5</button>
    <button
onclick="pressNumber(6)">6</button>
    <button onclick="pressOperator('-')">-
</button>
</div>
<div>
    <button
onclick="pressNumber(7)">7</button>
    <button
onclick="pressNumber(8)">8</button>
    <button
onclick="pressNumber(9)">9</button>
```

```
    <button
onclick="pressOperator('*')">*</button>
</div>
<div>
    <button
onclick="pressNumber(0)">0</button>
    <button
onclick="pressEquals()">=</button>
    <button
onclick="clearDisplay()">C</button>
    <button
onclick="pressOperator('/')">/</button>
</div>
<script src="app.js"></script>
```

2. **JavaScript Code** (app.js):

```javascript

let currentInput = '';
let previousInput = '';
let operator = null;

// Higher-order function to handle operations
function applyOperation(a, b, operator) {
    switch (operator) {
        case '+':
            return a + b;
        case '-':
```

227

```javascript
            return a - b;
        case '*':
            return a * b;
        case '/':
            return a / b;
        default:
            return b;
    }
}


// Currying to handle operations step by
step
const createOperation = operator => a => b
=> applyOperation(a, b, operator);


const add = createOperation('+');
const subtract = createOperation('-');
const multiply = createOperation('*');
const divide = createOperation('/');


// Compose    functions    for    chaining
operations
const calculator = (a, b, operator) => {
    const operations = {
        '+': add,
        '-': subtract,
        '*': multiply,
        '/': divide
    };
```

```javascript
        return operations[operator](a)(b);
};


// Handle number button press
function pressNumber(number) {
    currentInput += number;
    updateDisplay();
}


// Handle operator button press
function pressOperator(op) {
    if (currentInput === '') return;
    previousInput = currentInput;
    operator = op;
    currentInput = '';
}


// Handle equals button press
function pressEquals() {
    if    (previousInput    ===    ''    ||
currentInput === '') return;
    const          result          =
calculator(Number(previousInput),
Number(currentInput), operator);
    currentInput = result.toString();
    operator = null;
    previousInput = '';
    updateDisplay();
}
```

```
// Clear the display
function clearDisplay() {
    currentInput = '';
    previousInput = '';
    operator = null;
    updateDisplay();
}

// Update the display with current input
function updateDisplay() {

document.getElementById('display').value =
currentInput;
}
```

3. **Explanation**:

   o **Higher-order function**: The `applyOperation` function is a higher-order function because it takes the operator (as a string) and applies the corresponding operation to the operands.

   o **Currying**: The `createOperation` function is a curried function that generates a specific operation function (e.g., `add`, `subtract`, etc.) which can then be used to handle multiple steps of the calculation.

   o **Composition**: The `calculator` function is composed of several smaller functions (`add`, subtract, `multiply`, `divide`), allowing for easy chaining and handling of operations.

- o The calculator allows the user to input numbers, select operators, and calculate results using the equals button.

4. **How It Works**:

- o **Number buttons** append digits to the current input.

- o **Operator buttons** store the current input and operator, clearing the display for the next input.

- o **Equals button** performs the operation using the previously stored input and operator.

- o **Clear button** resets everything.

Summary

In this chapter, you:

- Explored **Functional Programming** concepts in JavaScript, including **higher-order functions**, **currying**, and **function composition**.

- Learned how to implement a **functional calculator** that uses these functional programming techniques to manage the state and perform operations.

- Discovered how **higher-order functions** allow you to create more flexible and reusable logic, while **currying** and **function composition** simplify handling complex tasks in a modular way.

By mastering functional programming principles, you can write more declarative, concise, and maintainable code in JavaScript, especially in scenarios requiring complex transformations or handling state across various operations.

CHAPTER 20

MODULES AND NAMESPACES

Understanding JavaScript Modules

In JavaScript, **modules** are used to break down large programs into smaller, more manageable pieces of code. Each module can contain its own variables, functions, and classes, and these can be shared between different parts of your application using the **export** and **import** mechanisms. This helps keep code organized, improves reusability, and avoids global namespace pollution.

1. **What are Modules?** A **module** in JavaScript is a file containing code that can be imported into other JavaScript files. A module helps avoid having all your code in a single file, making it easier to maintain and scale. Modules can export functions, objects, or values, and other parts of the application can import and use them as needed.

2. **Benefits of Using Modules**:
   - **Separation of concerns**: Code is organized into distinct files based on functionality.
   - **Reusability**: Once a module is created, it can be reused in other parts of the application.

233

- o **Maintainability**: Modularized code is easier to debug and maintain because each module has a clear purpose and scope.
- o **Avoiding global scope pollution**: Using modules prevents variables and functions from accidentally interfering with each other in the global scope.

Exporting and Importing Code

In JavaScript, modules are typically created using the `export` and `import` keywords. These keywords allow you to share and reuse code across different files.

1. **Exporting Code**:
   - o **Named Exports**: You can export multiple elements (functions, variables, etc.) from a module by giving each one a name.
   - o **Default Export**: You can export one item as the default export from a module, making it easier to import without specifying a name.

Example of Named Exports:

```javascript
// math.js
```

234

```
export const add = (a, b) => a + b;
export const subtract = (a, b) => a - b;
```

Example of Default Export:

```
javascript
```

```
// logger.js
const logMessage = (message) => {
    console.log(message);
};
```

```
export default logMessage;
```

2. **Importing Code**: Once you have exported code from a module, you can import it into another module.

Example of Importing Named Exports:

```
javascript
```

```
// main.js
import { add, subtract } from './math.js';
```

```
console.log(add(5, 3));     // Output: 8
console.log(subtract(5, 3));  // Output: 2
```

Example of Importing Default Export:

```
javascript
```

235

```
// main.js
import logMessage from './logger.js';

logMessage("Hello, world!");   // Output:
Hello, world!
```

3. **Renaming Imports**: When importing named exports, you can rename them for convenience using the `as` keyword.

Example:

```
javascript

// main.js
import { add as addition, subtract as subtraction } from './math.js';

console.log(addition(5, 3));  // Output: 8
console.log(subtraction(5,   3));       //
Output: 2
```

4. **Dynamic Imports**: JavaScript also supports dynamic imports using the `import()` function. This allows you to import modules on-demand rather than at the top of the file.

Example:

```javascript
import('./math.js').then(module => {
    console.log(module.add(5,  3));     // 
Output: 8
});
```

Real-world Example: Modularizing a Large Web App

Let's build a **modularized web app** to manage tasks, such as adding, removing, and displaying tasks. We will split the functionality into different modules for better organization and maintainability.

1. **HTML Structure** (index.html): We will have a simple HTML structure to display and manage tasks.

```html
<h1>Task Manager</h1>
<input      type="text"      id="taskInput"
placeholder="Enter a task">
<button           onclick="addTask()">Add
Task</button>

<ul id="taskList"></ul>
```

237

```
<script                          type="module"
src="app.js"></script>
```

2. **Task Management Modules**: We will create multiple modules to handle different aspects of the task manager.
   - **tasks.js**: Handles the task-related logic (adding, removing, and displaying tasks).
   - **ui.js**: Handles DOM manipulation (displaying tasks in the UI).

tasks.js:

```javascript

let tasks = [];

// Add a task
export const addTask = (task) => {
    tasks.push(task);
};

// Remove a task by index
export const removeTask = (index) => {
    tasks.splice(index, 1);
};

// Get all tasks
export const getTasks = () => {
    return tasks;
```

```
};
```

ui.js:

```javascript

import { getTasks, addTask, removeTask }
from './tasks.js';

// Render tasks in the UI
export const renderTasks = () => {
    const          taskList          =
document.getElementById('taskList');
    taskList.innerHTML = '';    // Clear
existing tasks

    const tasks = getTasks();
    tasks.forEach((task, index) => {
        const          li          =
document.createElement('li');
        li.textContent = task;
        li.onclick      =      ()      =>
removeTask(index);  // Click to remove task
        taskList.appendChild(li);
    });
};
```

3. **Main Application File** (app.js): The app.js file will tie everything together by importing the necessary modules and handling user interactions.

239

```javascript
javascript

import { addTask } from './tasks.js';
import { renderTasks } from './ui.js';

// Add a task from user input
export const addTaskFromInput = () => {
    const           taskInput           =
document.getElementById('taskInput');
    const task = taskInput.value.trim();

    if (task !== '') {
        addTask(task);
        renderTasks();  // Re-render tasks
after adding
    }

    taskInput.value = '';   // Clear the
input field
};

// Set up event listeners
document.querySelector('button').addEvent
Listener('click', addTaskFromInput);

// Initial render of tasks
renderTasks();
```

4. **How It Works**:

- o **tasks.js** manages the task data, including adding, removing, and retrieving tasks.
- o **ui.js** handles the display of tasks, interacting with the DOM to show the current list of tasks.
- o **app.js** serves as the central controller, managing the logic for adding tasks based on user input and rendering the task list on the screen.

5. **Explanation**:

- o **Modularization**: By splitting the functionality into separate modules (`tasks.js` and `ui.js`), the code becomes more organized and easier to maintain. The logic for tasks is in one place, and the UI-related code is in another.
- o **Importing and Exporting**: The functions from `tasks.js` and `ui.js` are exported and imported into `app.js` to be used throughout the application.

Summary

In this chapter, you:

- Learned about **JavaScript modules**, their importance in organizing and maintaining large applications, and how to use the `export` and `import` keywords to share functionality between files.

- Explored different **types of exports**: named exports and default exports.

- Built a **real-world example** of a **task manager application** that uses modules to handle task data and UI rendering separately.

Modularizing code with JavaScript modules helps maintain cleaner and more organized code, especially in large applications. By leveraging the power of **import** and **export**, you can create reusable, maintainable, and scalable applications.

CHAPTER 21

WORKING WITH REST APIS

Understanding APIs and HTTP Methods

An **API (Application Programming Interface)** is a set of rules and protocols that allow one software application to interact with another. In the context of web development, APIs are used to enable communication between different systems or services, such as a web app and a backend server.

A **REST API (Representational State Transfer)** is a common architecture for web APIs that is based on HTTP and works with standard HTTP methods like GET, POST, PUT, and DELETE. REST APIs are stateless, meaning each request is independent and does not rely on any previous request.

HTTP Methods:

- **GET**: Used to retrieve data from the server.
- **POST**: Used to send data to the server (often to create a new resource).
- **PUT**: Used to update an existing resource.
- **DELETE**: Used to remove a resource from the server.

Example: A RESTful API endpoint might look like this:

```bash
GET
https://api.weather.com/v1/current?city=London
```

This endpoint would fetch the current weather data for the city of London.

Common JSON Response Format:

Most modern APIs return data in **JSON (JavaScript Object Notation)** format, which is a lightweight, human-readable way to represent data.

Example Response:

```json
{
    "location": "London",
    "temperature": 18,
    "condition": "Clear",
    "humidity": 60
}
```

244

In this example, the response includes weather-related information such as the temperature, condition, and humidity for a given location.

Fetching and Displaying Data from an API

In JavaScript, we can interact with APIs using the **fetch()** function, which is built into modern browsers. fetch() allows you to make HTTP requests to a given URL and receive a response, typically in JSON format.

1. **Making a GET Request**: You can use fetch() to send a GET request to an API and retrieve data.

   Example:

   ```javascript
   fetch('https://api.weather.com/v1/current?city=London')
       .then(response => response.json()) // Parse the response as JSON
       .then(data => {
           console.log(data); // Use the data from the API
       })
       .catch(error => {
           console.log('Error:', error);
   ```

```
});
```

- o The `fetch()` function returns a **Promise** that resolves to the response object.
- o The `.json()` method is called on the response to parse the data into a JavaScript object.

2. **Handling Errors**: It's important to handle errors in case the API request fails (e.g., network issues, invalid responses).

Example:

```javascript

fetch('https://api.weather.com/v1/current
?city=London')
    .then(response => {
        if (!response.ok) {
            throw    new    Error('Network
response was not ok');
        }
        return response.json();
    })
    .then(data => {
        console.log(data);  // Use the data
from the API
    })
    .catch(error => {
```

```
        console.log('Error    fetching    the
weather data:', error);
    });
```

Real-world Example: Creating a Weather App Using an API

Let's create a **Weather App** that fetches weather data from an external weather API and displays it on a webpage. This app will allow the user to enter a city name and fetch the weather for that city.

1. **HTML Structure**: Create the basic structure of the weather app with input fields for the city name and a button to fetch the weather.

   html

   ```
   <h1>Weather App</h1>
   <input     type="text"     id="cityInput"
   placeholder="Enter city name">
   <button      onclick="getWeather()">Get
   Weather</button>

   <h2>Weather Information:</h2>
   <p id="weatherOutput">Please   enter   a  city
   name to get the weather.</p>

   <script src="app.js"></script>
   ```

2. **JavaScript Code** (app.js): The JavaScript code will use the fetch() function to get weather data from an external API and display it on the page.

Example of fetching weather data:

```javascript
const apiKey = 'your_api_key'; // Replace
with your API key
const                apiUrl                =
'https://api.openweathermap.org/data/2.5/
weather';


// Function to fetch weather data from the
API
function getWeather() {
    const            city             =
document.getElementById('cityInput').valu
e;
    if (!city) {

document.getElementById('weatherOutput').
textContent = 'Please enter a city name.';
        return;
    }


    // Construct the API URL with the city
and API key
```

248

```
    const              url              =
`${apiUrl}?q=${city}&appid=${apiKey}&unit
s=metric`;

    fetch(url)
        .then(response => {
            if (!response.ok) {
                throw new Error('City not
found');
            }
            return response.json();
        })
        .then(data => {
            // Extract relevant data from
the API response
            const       temperature      =
data.main.temp;
            const    weatherCondition    =
data.weather[0].description;
            const        humidity         =
data.main.humidity;

            //    Display    the    weather
information on the page
            const weatherOutput = `
            Temperature:
${temperature}°C
                <br>
```

```
                  Condition:
${weatherCondition}
                  <br>
                  Humidity: ${humidity}%
          `;
```

```
document.getElementById('weatherOutput').
innerHTML = weatherOutput;
        })
        .catch(error => {
            // Display an error message if
the city is not found or the API request
fails
```

```
document.getElementById('weatherOutput').
textContent = `Error: ${error.message}`;
        });
}
```

3. **Explanation**:

   o **User Input**: The user enters a city name into the input field, and when they click the "Get Weather" button, the `getWeather()` function is called.

   o **API Request**: The function constructs the API URL by appending the city name and API key to the base URL. It then uses `fetch()` to send a GET request to the weather API.

- o **Handling the Response**: The response is parsed as JSON, and the temperature, weather condition, and humidity are extracted and displayed on the webpage.
- o **Error Handling**: If the city is not found or there's an issue with the API request, an error message is displayed.

4. **Styling (Optional)**: To improve the user experience, you can add some CSS to style the app.

Example:

```css
body {
    font-family: Arial, sans-serif;
    padding: 20px;
}

input, button {
    padding: 10px;
    margin: 5px;
    font-size: 16px;
}

#weatherOutput {
    margin-top: 20px;
    font-size: 18px;
}
```

Summary

In this chapter, you:

- Learned about **REST APIs** and **HTTP methods**, and how to make HTTP requests using **JavaScript** to interact with APIs.
- Explored how to **fetch and display data** from an external API using the `fetch()` function and handle errors.
- Created a **real-world weather app** that fetches weather data from an external API and displays it on the webpage.

Working with APIs is essential in modern web development, as many applications rely on external data sources. By using **REST APIs**, you can integrate third-party services into your applications, offering dynamic and real-time data to your users.

CHAPTER 22

WEBSOCKETS AND REAL-TIME DATA

Introduction to WebSockets for Real-Time Communication

WebSockets are a protocol for establishing a persistent, bi-directional communication channel between a client (usually a web browser) and a server. Unlike traditional HTTP, which is request-response-based, WebSockets allow for real-time, two-way communication with minimal latency. This makes WebSockets ideal for building applications that require real-time updates, such as chat apps, live notifications, gaming apps, and collaborative tools.

How WebSockets Work:

1. **Handshake**: The connection begins with an HTTP request to the server. Once the server accepts the WebSocket protocol, the connection is "upgraded" from HTTP to WebSocket.

2. **Persistent Connection**: After the handshake, a full-duplex connection is established, meaning both the client and server can send and receive messages at any time.

3. **Low Latency**: Because WebSockets maintain an open connection, they allow for faster message exchanges, making them suitable for real-time applications.

4. **Event-driven**: The connection is event-driven, meaning messages can be sent and received asynchronously.

Advantages of WebSockets:

- **Real-Time Communication**: WebSockets are perfect for real-time applications like chat systems, stock price trackers, and multiplayer games.

- **Reduced Overhead**: Unlike HTTP, which opens a new connection for each request, WebSockets keep the connection open, reducing the overhead of creating and closing connections.

- **Two-Way Communication**: Both the client and the server can send messages to each other at any time.

Implementing Real-Time Features in Web Apps

To implement real-time features in a web application, we need to create a WebSocket server and client that can exchange messages.

1. **Setting Up the WebSocket Server**: You can set up a WebSocket server using various server technologies, such as **Node.js** with the `ws` package. WebSocket servers listen

for incoming WebSocket requests, process them, and broadcast messages to connected clients.

2. **Setting Up the WebSocket Client**: On the client-side (the browser), you use the `WebSocket` API to establish a connection to the server and send/receive messages.

Basic WebSocket Setup:

1. **Server-side (Node.js)**: First, you need to install the `ws` package to work with WebSockets in Node.js:

```bash
bash
```

```bash
npm install ws
```

WebSocket Server (server.js):

```javascript
javascript
```

```javascript
const WebSocket = require('ws');
const wss = new WebSocket.Server({ port: 8080 });

wss.on('connection', ws => {
    console.log('A        new        client
connected!');

    // Sending a message to the client
```

255

```
    ws.send('Welcome  to  the  WebSocket
server!');

    // Listening  for  messages  from  the
client
    ws.on('message', message => {
        console.log(`Received:
${message}`);
        // Broadcasting  the  received
message to all clients
        wss.clients.forEach(client => {
            if  (client  !==  ws  &&
client.readyState === WebSocket.OPEN) {
                client.send(message);
            }
        });
    });

    // Handling client disconnection
    ws.on('close', () => {
        console.log('A           client
disconnected');
    });
});

console.log('WebSocket  server  is  running
on ws://localhost:8080');
```

In this example, the WebSocket server listens on port `8080` and sends a welcome message to the client once a connection is established. It then listens for messages from clients and broadcasts those messages to all other connected clients.

2. **Client-side (Browser)**: The client uses the `WebSocket` API to connect to the WebSocket server and send/receive messages.

WebSocket Client (index.html):

```
html
```

```html
<!DOCTYPE html>
<html lang="en">
<head>
    <meta charset="UTF-8">
    <meta                     name="viewport"
content="width=device-width,      initial-
scale=1.0">
    <title>WebSocket Chat</title>
</head>
<body>
    <h1>WebSocket Chat</h1>
    <input  type="text"  id="messageInput"
placeholder="Enter message">
    <button
onclick="sendMessage()">Send</button>
```

257

```
<ul id="messages"></ul>

<script>
    // Connect to the WebSocket server
    const     socket     =     new
WebSocket('ws://localhost:8080');

    // When connection is established
    socket.addEventListener('open', ()
=> {
        console.log('Connected to the
WebSocket server');
    });

    // Listen for messages from the
server

socket.addEventListener('message',   event
=> {
        const     messageList     =
document.getElementById('messages');
        const     newMessage     =
document.createElement('li');
        newMessage.textContent     =
event.data;

messageList.appendChild(newMessage);
    });
```

```
// Send a message to the server
function sendMessage() {
    const        messageInput        =
document.getElementById('messageInput');
    const        message        =
messageInput.value;
    socket.send(message);  // Send
the message to the server
    messageInput.value = '';   //
Clear the input field
    }
</script>
</body>
</html>
```

o **Client-Side WebSocket**: The client uses the WebSocket API to connect to the WebSocket server at ws://localhost:8080. It sends messages to the server when the "Send" button is clicked, and listens for incoming messages from the server to display them in the chat.

Real-world Example: Building a Chat Application with WebSockets

In this real-world example, we will build a **simple chat application** that uses WebSockets for real-time communication.

259

When one user sends a message, it is immediately broadcasted to all connected clients.

1. **Server-Side WebSocket Setup**: As shown above, we set up the WebSocket server using Node.js and the `ws` package. The server listens for incoming messages and broadcasts them to all connected clients.

2. **Client-Side WebSocket Setup**: The client uses the WebSocket API to connect to the server and listen for incoming messages. When the user types a message and presses the "Send" button, the message is sent to the server, which then broadcasts it to all connected clients.

Here's an extended version of the **client-side HTML** to handle better formatting and UI updates:

```
html
```

```html
<!DOCTYPE html>
<html lang="en">
<head>
    <meta charset="UTF-8">
    <meta                      name="viewport"
content="width=device-width,      initial-
scale=1.0">
    <title>WebSocket Chat App</title>
    <style>
        body {
```

```css
            font-family:    Arial,    sans-
serif;
            padding: 20px;
        }
        input[type="text"] {
            width: 300px;
            padding: 10px;
            margin-right: 10px;
        }
        button {
            padding: 10px;
            font-size: 16px;
        }
        #messages {
            margin-top: 20px;
            list-style-type: none;
            padding: 0;
        }
        #messages li {
            background-color: #f1f1f1;
            margin-bottom: 10px;
            padding: 10px;
            border-radius: 5px;
            width: 300px;
        }
    </style>
</head>
<body>
    <h1>WebSocket Chat Application</h1>
```

261

```
<input type="text" id="messageInput"
placeholder="Type your message...">
<button
onclick="sendMessage()">Send</button>

<ul id="messages"></ul>

<script>
    // Establish a WebSocket
connection
    const socket = new
WebSocket('ws://localhost:8080');

    // When the connection is
established
    socket.addEventListener('open', ()
=> {
        console.log('Connected to the
WebSocket server');
    });

    // Display incoming messages

socket.addEventListener('message', event
=> {
        const messageList =
document.getElementById('messages');
        const newMessage =
document.createElement('li');
```

```
            newMessage.textContent      =
event.data;

messageList.appendChild(newMessage);
        });

        // Send a message to the server
        function sendMessage() {
            const      messageInput      =
document.getElementById('messageInput');
            const        message        =
messageInput.value;
            if (message.trim() !== '') {
                socket.send(message);    //
Send the message
                messageInput.value = '';
// Clear the input field
            }
        }
    </script>
</body>
</html>
```

Summary

In this chapter, you:

- **Learned about WebSockets**, a protocol that allows for real-time, bi-directional communication between clients and servers.
- **Explored how WebSockets differ** from traditional HTTP communication, offering low-latency and persistent connections.
- **Implemented real-time features** in web apps using WebSockets, including creating a simple chat application where users can send and receive messages in real-time.
- **Understood how WebSocket servers** and **clients interact**, and how WebSocket-based communication enables efficient, real-time interactions in modern web applications.

WebSockets are an essential tool for building interactive, real-time web applications such as chat systems, notifications, and collaborative tools, and they are widely used in various modern web development scenarios.

CHAPTER 23

JAVASCRIPT AND THE BROWSER: WEB SECURITY ESSENTIALS

Understanding Common Web Vulnerabilities (XSS, CSRF)

In web development, security is a critical concern, as vulnerabilities can lead to data breaches, unauthorized access, and malicious attacks. Two of the most common vulnerabilities in web applications are **Cross-Site Scripting (XSS)** and **Cross-Site Request Forgery (CSRF)**. Understanding these vulnerabilities is essential for building secure web applications.

1. Cross-Site Scripting (XSS)

XSS occurs when an attacker injects malicious scripts into a webpage that is viewed by other users. These scripts run in the browser of the victim, potentially allowing attackers to steal session cookies, redirect users to malicious websites, or perform actions on behalf of the user without their consent.

There are three main types of XSS attacks:

265

- **Stored XSS**: The attacker injects a malicious script into a website's database (e.g., a forum post or comment), and when another user views the page, the script executes.
- **Reflected XSS**: The malicious script is embedded in a URL and executed when the user clicks on a link or submits a form.
- **DOM-based XSS**: The attack targets the Document Object Model (DOM) directly in the browser, typically through client-side JavaScript.

How to prevent XSS:

- **Sanitize input**: Ensure that user inputs (such as comments, form fields, etc.) are sanitized to remove any potentially dangerous characters (like <, >, and &).
- **Use secure libraries**: Use libraries like `DOMPurify` to sanitize user inputs and prevent script injections.
- **Content Security Policy (CSP)**: Implement CSP headers to restrict the sources from which scripts can be loaded and executed.

2. Cross-Site Request Forgery (CSRF)

CSRF occurs when a malicious website tricks a user into making an unwanted request to a different website where the user is authenticated. This can allow attackers to perform actions on behalf of the user without their consent, such as changing account settings or making purchases.

How CSRF works:

- An attacker sends a malicious link or request to a victim who is logged into a target site.
- If the victim clicks on the link, the browser sends a request to the target site using the victim's authenticated session, which the server processes as a legitimate request.

How to prevent CSRF:

- **Anti-CSRF tokens**: Use tokens to verify that the request comes from a legitimate user and not a malicious third-party. These tokens are unique per session and must be included in every form or API request.
- **SameSite cookies**: Set the `SameSite` attribute of cookies to `Strict` or `Lax` to restrict cookies from being sent with cross-site requests.

Secure Data Handling and Authentication

When dealing with sensitive data, it is essential to follow best practices for data handling and authentication. These practices help protect user information and ensure secure interactions between users and your web application.

1. Handling Sensitive Data:

- **Encryption**: Always encrypt sensitive data both in transit (using **HTTPS**) and at rest (using encryption algorithms like AES).

- **Avoid storing passwords**: Never store plaintext passwords in your database. Always hash passwords using secure algorithms like **bcrypt** or **Argon2**.

- **Token-based authentication**: Use **JWT (JSON Web Tokens)** for secure user authentication, as they are compact, self-contained, and provide an easy way to manage session tokens without storing session data on the server.

2. Secure Authentication:

- **Multi-Factor Authentication (MFA)**: Implement multi-factor authentication (MFA) to require users to verify their identity using something they have (like a mobile device) in addition to their password.

- **Password Policies**: Enforce strong password policies, such as requiring a mix of letters, numbers, and special characters, to make passwords harder to guess or crack.

- **Session Management**: Properly manage sessions by setting secure cookie attributes (e.g., `HttpOnly`, `Secure`, `SameSite`) and ensuring sessions are invalidated after logout.

3. HTTPS (SSL/TLS):

- **Always use HTTPS**: Secure your website by using HTTPS for encrypted communication between the client and the server. This prevents man-in-the-middle attacks and ensures that the data cannot be intercepted during transmission.

Real-world Example: Building a Secure Login System

Let's build a **secure login system** that uses **JWT (JSON Web Tokens)** for authentication and implements security best practices like **password hashing**, **anti-CSRF tokens**, and **session management**.

Step 1: Backend Setup (Node.js with Express)

1. **Install Dependencies**:

   bash

   ```
   npm install express bcryptjs jsonwebtoken
   cookie-parser dotenv
   ```

2. **Backend Code (server.js)**: The backend will handle user registration, login, and token-based authentication.

   javascript

269

```javascript
const express = require('express');
const bcrypt = require('bcryptjs');
const jwt = require('jsonwebtoken');
const cookieParser = require('cookie-
parser');
const dotenv = require('dotenv');
dotenv.config();

const app = express();
app.use(express.json());
app.use(cookieParser());

const users = []; // In-memory user storage
for demonstration

// JWT Secret key (store it securely in
environment variables)
const JWT_SECRET = process.env.JWT_SECRET;

// Register endpoint
app.post('/register', async (req, res) =>
{
    const { username, password } =
req.body;
    const hashedPassword = await
bcrypt.hash(password, 10);
```

```
    // Save the user to the "database" (in-
memory array)
    users.push({    username,    password:
hashedPassword });
    res.status(201).send('User
registered');
});

// Login endpoint
app.post('/login', async (req, res) => {
    const   {   username,   password   }   =
req.body;
    const user = users.find(u => u.username
=== username);

    if        (!user        ||        !(await
bcrypt.compare(password,   user.password)))
{
        return
res.status(401).send('Invalid
credentials');
    }

    // Generate JWT token
    const token = jwt.sign({ username },
JWT_SECRET, { expiresIn: '1h' });

    // Send token as a cookie (HttpOnly and
Secure)
```

271

```javascript
  res.cookie('token', token, { httpOnly:
true, secure: true, sameSite: 'Strict' });
    res.send('Logged in successfully');
});

// Protected endpoint
app.get('/profile', authenticateJWT, (req,
res) => {
    res.send('This is your profile data');
});

// Middleware for authenticating JWT
function authenticateJWT(req, res, next) {
    const token = req.cookies.token;
    if          (!token)          return
res.status(403).send('Access denied');

    jwt.verify(token,   JWT_SECRET,   (err,
user) => {
        if          (err)          return
res.status(403).send('Invalid token');
        req.user = user;
        next();
    });
}

// Start server
app.listen(3000, () => {
```

```
    console.log('Server    is    running    on
http://localhost:3000');
});
```

Step 2: Frontend Setup (HTML + JavaScript)

1. **Frontend Code (index.html)**: This simple frontend allows users to register, log in, and view their profile.

```html
html

<h1>Secure Login System</h1>

<div>
    <h2>Register</h2>
    <input                     type="text"
id="registerUsername"
placeholder="Username">
    <input                  type="password"
id="registerPassword"
placeholder="Password">
    <button
onclick="register()">Register</button>
</div>

<div>
    <h2>Login</h2>
    <input type="text" id="loginUsername"
placeholder="Username">
```

273

```
    <input                      type="password"
id="loginPassword" placeholder="Password">
    <button
onclick="login()">Login</button>
</div>

<div>
    <h2>Profile</h2>
    <button    onclick="viewProfile()">View
Profile</button>
</div>

<script>
    async function register() {
        const         username         =
document.getElementById('registerUsername
').value;
        const        password         =
document.getElementById('registerPassword
').value;

        const    response    =    await
fetch('http://localhost:3000/register', {
            method: 'POST',
            headers:  {  'Content-Type':
'application/json' },
            body:         JSON.stringify({
username, password })
        });
```

```
       if (response.ok) {
           alert('User          registered
successfully');
       } else {
           alert('Error          registering
user');
       }
    }


   async function login() {
       const          username          =
document.getElementById('loginUsername').
value;
       const          password          =
document.getElementById('loginPassword').
value;


       const     response     =     await
fetch('http://localhost:3000/login', {
           method: 'POST',
           headers:   {   'Content-Type':
'application/json' },
           body:          JSON.stringify({
username, password })
       });


       if (response.ok) {
           alert('Login successful');
```

275

```
        } else {
            alert('Error logging in');
        }
    }


    async function viewProfile() {
        const     response     =     await
fetch('http://localhost:3000/profile', {
            method: 'GET',
            credentials: 'include' // Send
cookies with the request
        });

        if (response.ok) {
            alert('Profile              data
retrieved');
        } else {
            alert('Access denied');
        }
    }
</script>
```

Summary

In this chapter, you:

- **Learned about common web vulnerabilities**, such as **XSS** and **CSRF**, and how to mitigate them.

- **Explored secure data handling** techniques like password hashing, token-based authentication (JWT), and using HTTPS.
- **Built a secure login system** that demonstrates the use of **JWT** for authentication, **cookie management** for sessions, and basic **password hashing** using bcrypt.

Security is an essential aspect of web development, and by understanding and implementing these practices, you can protect your users' data and build secure applications.

CHAPTER 24

PROGRESSIVE WEB APPS (PWAS)

What Are PWAs and Why They Matter

A **Progressive Web App (PWA)** is a type of web application that offers a native mobile app-like experience while still being delivered through the web. PWAs combine the best features of both web and mobile applications. They are designed to work on any platform, regardless of the device or operating system, offering a seamless experience across desktops, tablets, and smartphones.

PWAs are built with modern web technologies and are intended to provide:

- **Reliability**: They work in any environment, even with poor or no internet connection.
- **Performance**: They load quickly, providing fast interactions with users.
- **Engagement**: PWAs can be added to the home screen, work offline, and push notifications, making them highly engaging.

Why PWAs Matter:

- **Offline Capabilities**: PWAs work seamlessly offline or with low connectivity, enhancing user experience in regions with poor internet access.

- **Improved Performance**: They offer a smoother, faster experience compared to traditional web apps by caching important assets and data.

- **Mobile-First Approach**: PWAs prioritize mobile responsiveness and provide a native-like experience.

- **Cross-Platform Support**: PWAs can run on any device, whether it's Android, iOS, Windows, or macOS.

- **No App Store Dependency**: Unlike traditional mobile apps, PWAs do not require approval from an app store, making them quicker and easier to deploy.

Service Workers and Caching for Offline Use

One of the core technologies behind PWAs is **Service Workers**. A service worker is a special type of JavaScript file that runs in the background, separate from the web page. It enables features that don't need a web page or user interaction, such as caching assets, background syncing, and push notifications.

What Is a Service Worker?

A service worker is a JavaScript file that operates between the browser and the network, allowing you to control how network requests are handled. It is used primarily for:

- **Offline caching**: Allowing a web app to load and function offline by caching files and assets.
- **Background sync**: Ensuring that requests are completed even if the user is not connected to the network.
- **Push notifications**: Sending notifications to users even when they are not actively using the app.

How Service Workers Work:

1. **Install**: The service worker is installed and set up to manage caches.
2. **Activate**: The service worker is activated and starts handling requests.
3. **Fetch**: The service worker intercepts network requests, allowing it to serve cached assets or retrieve new data from the network.

Service Worker Caching for Offline Use:

To enable offline use, service workers cache assets like HTML files, JavaScript, CSS, images, and API responses, allowing the app to continue functioning without an active internet connection.

Example:

javascript

```javascript
// Register the service worker
if ('serviceWorker' in navigator) {
    navigator.serviceWorker.register('/service-
worker.js')
        .then(registration => {
            console.log('Service        Worker
registered with scope:', registration.scope);
        })
        .catch(error => {
            console.log('Service        Worker
registration failed:', error);
        });
}
```

Service Worker Implementation (service-worker.js):

javascript

```javascript
const CACHE_NAME = 'my-cache-v1';
const URLS_TO_CACHE = [
    '/',
    '/index.html',
    '/styles.css',
    '/app.js',
    '/images/logo.png'
];
```

```javascript
// Install event: Cache important files
self.addEventListener('install', event => {
    event.waitUntil(
        caches.open(CACHE_NAME)
            .then(cache                  =>
cache.addAll(URLS_TO_CACHE))
    );
});


// Activate event: Remove old caches
self.addEventListener('activate', event => {
    const cacheWhitelist = [CACHE_NAME];
    event.waitUntil(
        caches.keys()
            .then(cacheNames => {
                return Promise.all(
                    cacheNames.map(cacheName  =>
{
                        if
(!cacheWhitelist.includes(cacheName)) {
                            return
caches.delete(cacheName);
                        }
                    })
                );
            })
    );
});
```

```
// Fetch event: Serve cached content when offline
self.addEventListener('fetch', event => {
    event.respondWith(
        caches.match(event.request)
            .then(response => {
                // Return cached response if
available, otherwise fetch from network
                return         response         ||
fetch(event.request);
            })
    );
});
```

- **Installing the Service Worker**: The service worker is installed when the app is loaded. During installation, it caches key assets.

- **Activation**: On activation, the service worker cleans up old caches and ensures that only the current cache version is used.

- **Fetching Data**: The service worker intercepts network requests, and it serves cached files when the user is offline, ensuring the app works without a network connection.

Real-world Example: Turning a Static Website into a PWA

Let's walk through turning a simple static website into a **Progressive Web App (PWA)** by adding **Service Workers** and enabling **offline functionality**.

1. **Create the Static Website**: First, you need a basic static website with some HTML, CSS, and JavaScript.

   index.html:

   html

   ```
   <!DOCTYPE html>
   <html lang="en">
   <head>
       <meta charset="UTF-8">
       <meta                  name="viewport"
   content="width=device-width,        initial-
   scale=1.0">
       <title>My PWA</title>
       <link                rel="stylesheet"
   href="styles.css">
   </head>
   <body>
       <h1>Welcome  to  My  Progressive  Web
   App</h1>
       <p>This  is  a  simple  static  website
   turned into a PWA!</p>
   ```

```
    <script src="app.js"></script>
</body>
</html>
```

styles.css:

```
css


body {
    font-family: Arial, sans-serif;
    text-align: center;
}
```

app.js:

```
javascript


console.log('PWA JavaScript Loaded!');
```

2. **Add the `manifest.json` File**: A **manifest file** is required to define your PWA's appearance and behavior on the home screen of a mobile device. It specifies things like the app's name, icons, background color, and display settings.

manifest.json:

```
json


{
```

285

```
"name": "My PWA",
"short_name": "PWA",
"description": "A simple progressive
web app",
"start_url": "/",
"display": "standalone",
"background_color": "#ffffff",
"theme_color": "#000000",
"icons": [
    {
        "src":             "icons/icon-
192x192.png",
        "sizes": "192x192",
        "type": "image/png"
    },
    {
        "src":             "icons/icon-
512x512.png",
        "sizes": "512x512",
        "type": "image/png"
    }
  ]
}
```

3. **Register the Service Worker**: In your **app.js** file, add the code to register the service worker and enable caching.

```javascript
javascript

if ('serviceWorker' in navigator) {
```

```
    window.addEventListener('load', () =>
{

navigator.serviceWorker.register('/servic
e-worker.js')
            .then(registration => {
                console.log('Service
Worker registered:', registration);
            })
            .catch(error => {
                console.log('Service
Worker registration failed:', error);
            });
    });
}
```

4. **Add the Service Worker**: Create a `service-worker.js` file to handle caching and offline functionality.

   service-worker.js:

   javascript

```
const CACHE_NAME = 'my-pwa-cache-v1';
const URLS_TO_CACHE = [
    '/',
    '/index.html',
    '/styles.css',
```

```
    '/app.js',
    '/icons/icon-192x192.png',
    '/icons/icon-512x512.png'
];

self.addEventListener('install', event =>
{
    event.waitUntil(
        caches.open(CACHE_NAME)
            .then(cache                  =>
cache.addAll(URLS_TO_CACHE))
    );
});

self.addEventListener('activate', event =>
{
    const cacheWhitelist = [CACHE_NAME];
    event.waitUntil(
        caches.keys()
            .then(cacheNames => {
                return Promise.all(

cacheNames.map(cacheName => {
                        if
(!cacheWhitelist.includes(cacheName)) {
                            return
caches.delete(cacheName);
                        }
                    })
```

```
                    );
                })
        );
});


self.addEventListener('fetch', event => {
    event.respondWith(
        caches.match(event.request)
            .then(response => response ||
fetch(event.request))
    );
});
```

5. **Testing Your PWA**:

o **Test Offline**: Once the service worker is in place, you can test the offline functionality by disconnecting your internet and refreshing the page. The website should still load using the cached assets.

o **Add to Home Screen**: To make your app a true PWA, test adding it to the home screen on a mobile device. This will install the app on your device and allow users to use it without a browser address bar.

Summary

In this chapter, you:

- Learned about **Progressive Web Apps (PWAs)** and their advantages, such as offline functionality, better performance, and the ability to be installed on the home screen of mobile devices.
- Explored **Service Workers** and their role in enabling caching, offline use, and background tasks in PWAs.
- **Transformed a simple static website into a PWA**, using key components like the manifest file and service workers to make it functional offline and installable on mobile devices.

PWAs are revolutionizing web development by providing a native app-like experience on the web. By adding these features to your websites, you can significantly improve user engagement and retention.

CHAPTER 25

TESTING AND DEBUGGING JAVASCRIPT APPLICATIONS

Introduction to Unit Testing and Test Frameworks (Jest, Mocha)

Unit testing is a software testing technique where individual units or components of a software are tested in isolation to ensure that they perform as expected. For JavaScript applications, unit tests are essential to verify that individual functions or methods work correctly, especially as applications grow in size and complexity.

Unit testing helps ensure that:

- **Components behave as expected** in isolation.
- **Bugs are caught early** in the development process.
- **Refactoring** doesn't break existing functionality.

Popular JavaScript Testing Frameworks:

1. **Jest**: Jest is a widely-used JavaScript testing framework developed by Facebook. It's simple to set up, provides built-in test runners, and supports snapshot testing. Jest is commonly used with React applications but can be used with any JavaScript codebase.

291

Features:

- o Zero configuration (works out-of-the-box).
- o Built-in mocking and spying.
- o Snapshot testing.
- o Easy asynchronous testing.
- o Built-in code coverage.

Example:

```javascript
test('adds 1 + 2 to equal 3', () => {
    expect(1 + 2).toBe(3);
});
```

2. **Mocha**: Mocha is a flexible testing framework that works well with various assertion libraries (like Chai) and test reporters. It's highly configurable and widely used in Node.js applications.

Features:

- o Supports both **TDD (Test-Driven Development)** and **BDD (Behavior-Driven Development)**.
- o Asynchronous testing support.
- o Can be paired with other tools like **Chai** for assertions.

292

Example:

```javascript

const assert = require('chai').assert;

describe('Addition', function() {
    it('should return 3 when 1 + 2 is added', function() {
        assert.equal(1 + 2, 3);
    });
});
```

3. **Choosing Between Jest and Mocha**:

   o **Jest**: Great for React and modern JavaScript applications with minimal setup.

   o **Mocha**: More flexible and suitable for projects that require customized setups or specific integration with other libraries.

Writing Testable Code and Debugging Tools

Writing testable code means structuring your code in a way that makes it easy to test. This involves writing **small, modular functions** with **single responsibilities**.

Principles of Writing Testable Code:

1. **Small Functions**: Functions should do one thing and do it well. This makes them easier to test.

   Example:

   ```javascript
   // Testable function
   const add = (a, b) => a + b;
   ```

2. **Pure Functions**: Pure functions always return the same output given the same inputs and have no side effects (e.g., modifying global state). Pure functions are easy to test because they don't depend on or modify external variables.

   Example:

   ```javascript
   const multiply = (a, b) => a * b;   // Pure function
   ```

3. **Avoiding Side Effects**: Avoid code that interacts with external systems (like the DOM, APIs, or databases) inside your core logic. Instead, use mock functions or abstract these interactions to make the logic easier to test.

4. **Separation of Concerns**: Separate business logic from presentation or network logic. This makes the core logic (business rules) easier to test in isolation.

Using Debugging Tools:

1. **Console Logging**: Use `console.log()` to output intermediate values and track the flow of execution in your code.

2. **Breakpoints and Inspecting Variables**: Most modern browsers come with built-in developer tools. Use breakpoints in the **Debugger** tab to pause the execution of your code and inspect variables, call stacks, and network requests.

3. **The `debugger` Statement**: You can insert the `debugger` statement in your JavaScript code to pause execution and enter the debugger at that point.

   Example:

```javascript

const result = add(2, 3);
debugger;   // Pause here and inspect the
result in the browser's developer tools
```

4. **Test Coverage**: Many testing tools, like Jest, provide **coverage reports** that show which parts of your code are

being tested and which are not. This helps identify areas that need more test coverage.

Real-world Example: Writing Tests for a Todo App

Let's demonstrate how to write unit tests for a simple **Todo App** that allows users to add and remove tasks. We'll use **Jest** to write and run the tests.

Step 1: Building the Todo App Logic

Start by writing the basic logic for the Todo App. The app should allow tasks to be added and removed.

todo.js:

```javascript
let todos = [];

const addTodo = (task) => {
    if (!task) throw new Error('Task cannot be empty');
    todos.push(task);
};

const removeTodo = (task) => {
    const index = todos.indexOf(task);
```

```
    if (index !== -1) {
        todos.splice(index, 1);
    }
};

const getTodos = () => todos;

module.exports = { addTodo, removeTodo, getTodos
};
```

- **addTodo**: Adds a task to the `todos` array.
- **removeTodo**: Removes a task from the `todos` array.
- **getTodos**: Returns the list of current tasks.

Step 2: Writing Unit Tests

Now, let's write some tests for the above logic. We will test if the tasks are being correctly added and removed.

todo.test.js:

```
javascript

const { addTodo, removeTodo, getTodos } =
require('./todo');

describe('Todo App', () => {
    beforeEach(() => {
        // Reset the todos array before each test
```

297

```
        global.todos = [];
    });

    test('should add a todo', () => {
        addTodo('Learn Jest');
        expect(getTodos()).toEqual(['Learn
Jest']);
    });

    test('should not add an empty todo', () => {
        expect(() => addTodo('')).toThrow('Task
cannot be empty');
    });

    test('should remove a todo', () => {
        addTodo('Learn Jest');
        removeTodo('Learn Jest');
        expect(getTodos()).toEqual([]);
    });

    test('should not remove a non-existent todo',
() => {
        addTodo('Learn Jest');
        removeTodo('Non-existent task');
        expect(getTodos()).toEqual(['Learn
Jest']);
    });
});
```

Explanation of Tests:

1. **beforeEach**: This function is executed before each test. It ensures that the `todos` array is reset to an empty state, so tests don't interfere with each other.

2. **Test for adding a todo**: The test checks that a task is successfully added to the `todos` array.

3. **Test for invalid task input**: This test verifies that trying to add an empty task throws an error.

4. **Test for removing a todo**: This test verifies that a task is removed correctly from the `todos` array.

5. **Test for removing a non-existent todo**: This test checks that attempting to remove a task that doesn't exist does not affect the `todos` array.

Step 3: Running the Tests

To run the tests, execute the following command in the terminal:

```bash
bash
```

```bash
npx jest
```

Jest will run the tests, and you'll see output like this:

```csharp
csharp
```

```
PASS  ./todo.test.js
```

299

```
Todo App
    ✓ should add a todo (3 ms)
    ✓ should not add an empty todo (1 ms)
    ✓ should remove a todo (1 ms)
    ✓ should not remove a non-existent todo (1
ms)
```

Summary

In this chapter, you:

- **Learned about unit testing** and testing frameworks like **Jest** and **Mocha**. These tools help ensure that individual components of your application work as expected.
- **Explored how to write testable code**, focusing on small, pure functions that are easy to test and debug.
- **Built and tested a simple Todo app**, where you wrote unit tests for adding and removing tasks, ensuring that the app logic was functioning correctly.
- **Understood debugging tools**, such as `console.log()`, breakpoints, and the `debugger` statement, which help track down issues and improve the development process.

Testing is a crucial part of the development workflow that helps ensure your application behaves correctly and reliably as it grows. By adopting testing early in your development process, you can

300

catch bugs early, improve maintainability, and make your code more robust.

CHAPTER 26

JAVASCRIPT FRAMEWORKS: REACT.JS OVERVIEW

Introduction to React and Its Ecosystem

React is one of the most popular JavaScript libraries for building user interfaces, primarily for single-page applications (SPAs). Developed by **Facebook**, React allows developers to create reusable UI components and manage state efficiently. It has become a cornerstone of modern web development, and its ecosystem is vast, offering powerful tools for building dynamic, responsive web apps.

Key Features of React:

- **Component-Based Architecture**: React encourages building applications by breaking down the UI into small, reusable components. Each component manages its own state and logic.
- **Declarative Syntax**: React uses a declarative approach to define how the UI should look based on the state, making it easy to understand and maintain.

- **Virtual DOM**: React creates a virtual representation of the real DOM in memory. When the state of a component changes, React efficiently updates only the necessary parts of the actual DOM, improving performance.
- **Unidirectional Data Flow**: React uses a one-way data flow, making it easier to manage and debug state changes.

React Ecosystem:

- **React Router**: A routing library for handling navigation in SPAs.
- **React Redux**: A state management library for managing global state in larger applications.
- **React Developer Tools**: A browser extension for debugging React applications, providing insights into the component tree and state changes.
- **React Native**: A framework that allows developers to build native mobile applications using React.

Building Dynamic Components with React

In React, the user interface is built using **components**, which are JavaScript functions or classes that define how a portion of the UI should appear. Components can be either **functional** or **class-based**, but functional components are becoming more popular due

303

to the introduction of **React Hooks**, which allow functional components to manage state and side effects.

Creating a Functional Component:

A functional component is a JavaScript function that returns JSX (JavaScript XML) to render the UI.

Example:

```javascript
import React from 'react';

const Welcome = ({ name }) => {
    return <h1>Hello, {name}!</h1>;
};

export default Welcome;
```

- **JSX**: React uses JSX, a syntax extension that looks similar to HTML, to describe the UI. JSX gets transformed into JavaScript function calls, allowing React to update the UI dynamically.

State and Event Handling:

React provides a `useState` hook for managing state within functional components. The `useState` hook allows you to define state variables and update them within your component.

Example (Counter Component):

```javascript
import React, { useState } from 'react';

const Counter = () => {
    const [count, setCount] = useState(0);

    const increment = () => {
        setCount(count + 1);
    };

    return (
        <div>
            <p>Count: {count}</p>
            <button
onClick={increment}>Increment</button>
        </div>
    );
};

export default Counter;
```

- **useState**: This hook initializes the `count` variable with a value of `0` and provides a function `setCount` to update it.
- **Event Handling**: The `onClick` event handler listens for user clicks and updates the state when the button is pressed.

Real-world Example: Creating a Dynamic Todo App with React

Let's walk through creating a **dynamic Todo app** using React. The app will allow users to add, delete, and toggle tasks as completed.

Step 1: Setting Up React:

If you haven't already set up a React project, you can do so using **Create React App**, a tool that sets up a new React project with all the necessary configurations.

1. **Install Create React App**:

bash

```
npx create-react-app todo-app
cd todo-app
npm start
```

2. This will create a new React project and start a development server at `http://localhost:3000`.

Step 2: Creating Components:

We'll create a `TodoApp` component that contains the state and methods to manage the tasks.

TodoApp.js:

```javascript
import React, { useState } from 'react';
import TodoItem from './TodoItem';  // Importing
the TodoItem component

const TodoApp = () => {
    const [tasks, setTasks] = useState([]);
    const [newTask, setNewTask] = useState('');

    const handleAddTask = () => {
        if (newTask.trim() !== '') {
            setTasks([...tasks,          {          id:
Date.now(), text: newTask, completed: false }]);
            setNewTask('');
        }
    };

    const handleToggleTask = (id) => {
```

307

```
        setTasks(
            tasks.map(task =>
                task.id === id ? { ...task,
completed: !task.completed } : task
            )
        );
    };


    const handleDeleteTask = (id) => {
        setTasks(tasks.filter(task => task.id
!== id));
    };


    return (
        <div>
            <h1>Todo App</h1>
            <input
                type="text"
                value={newTask}
                onChange={(e)             =>
setNewTask(e.target.value)}
                placeholder="Enter a new task"
            />
            <button onClick={handleAddTask}>Add
Task</button>
            <ul>
                {tasks.map(task => (
                    <TodoItem
                        key={task.id}
```

```
                    task={task}
                    onToggle={()            =>
handleToggleTask(task.id)}
                    onDelete={()            =>
handleDeleteTask(task.id)}
                  />
                ))}
            </ul>
        </div>
    );
};

export default TodoApp;
```

- **State**: The `TodoApp` component has two pieces of state: `tasks` (an array of todo items) and `newTask` (the input value for the new task).
- **Methods**: The component has methods for adding, toggling, and deleting tasks.
- **Rendering**: The `tasks` array is mapped to a list of `TodoItem` components.

Step 3: Creating the TodoItem Component:

Now, let's create a `TodoItem` component that will display individual todo tasks.

TodoItem.js:

```javascript

import React from 'react';

const TodoItem = ({ task, onToggle, onDelete }) => {
    return (
        <li style={{ textDecoration: task.completed ? 'line-through' : 'none' }}>
            <span onClick={onToggle} style={{ cursor: 'pointer' }}>
                {task.text}
            </span>
            <button onClick={onDelete}>Delete</button>
        </li>
    );
};

export default TodoItem;
```

- **Rendering a Todo**: The `TodoItem` component displays the task text. If the task is marked as completed, the text is styled with a line-through.
- **Event Handlers**: The `onToggle` and `onDelete` props allow the parent `TodoApp` component to toggle and delete tasks.

Step 4: Running the Todo App:

Now, if you run the app using `npm start`, you should be able to:

- Add new tasks.
- Toggle tasks as completed by clicking on them.
- Delete tasks using the delete button.

Summary

In this chapter, you:

- **Learned about React** and its ecosystem, including its component-based architecture, JSX, and use of state and props.
- **Built a dynamic Todo app** in React that allows users to add, toggle, and delete tasks.
- **Explored React's declarative syntax** and how it helps in managing UI changes efficiently.

React is a powerful tool for building modern, interactive web applications. By using components and hooks like `useState`, React allows you to manage application state in a clean and scalable way, making it easier to develop and maintain complex UIs.

CHAPTER 27

BUILDING FULL-STACK WEB APPLICATIONS WITH JAVASCRIPT

Full-Stack Development with JavaScript (Node.js, Express, MongoDB)

Full-stack development refers to the development of both the **front-end** (client-side) and **back-end** (server-side) of a web application. With **JavaScript**, you can use the same language for both the front-end and back-end, which makes it easier to build, manage, and maintain your application.

In this chapter, we will cover the essential tools and technologies for building a full-stack web application using **Node.js**, **Express**, and **MongoDB**. These tools allow you to handle server-side logic, routing, database interaction, and client-side rendering with one language: JavaScript.

What Is Full-Stack Development?

- **Front-end (Client-side)**: This is the user interface of the application. It is typically built using HTML, CSS, and

312

JavaScript, and it communicates with the back-end to fetch data and display it to the user.

- **Back-end (Server-side)**: This is the server that handles requests from the front-end, processes data, interacts with the database, and sends the response back to the client.

- **Database**: A storage system for your application's data. For this example, we'll use **MongoDB**, a NoSQL database that stores data in a flexible, JSON-like format.

Key Technologies:

1. **Node.js**: A JavaScript runtime built on Chrome's V8 engine. It allows you to run JavaScript code on the server-side.

2. **Express.js**: A minimal web framework for Node.js. It helps manage routing and handling HTTP requests.

3. **MongoDB**: A NoSQL database that stores data in a flexible format called BSON, which is similar to JSON. It's great for applications that require flexibility in their data models.

Building and Deploying a Full-Stack Web Application

1. Setting Up Your Development Environment

Before we start building, let's set up the environment:

- **Node.js**: Ensure you have Node.js installed on your system. You can download and install it from the official website: https://nodejs.org.
- **MongoDB**: You can use MongoDB locally or use a cloud-based version like **MongoDB Atlas** for easier deployment.
- **Text Editor**: Use an editor like **VS Code** or any editor you're comfortable with.

Once the environment is set up, you can start by initializing a **Node.js project** using npm (Node Package Manager):

bash

```
mkdir blog-app
cd blog-app
npm init -y  # Initializes a Node.js project
```

2. Installing Dependencies

You'll need to install the following dependencies for building the back-end:

- **Express**: For handling HTTP requests and routing.
- **Mongoose**: An ODM (Object Data Modeling) library for MongoDB, which helps manage data models.
- **Body-parser**: Middleware to parse incoming request bodies.

- **EJS**: A templating engine for rendering views in the front-end.

Install the dependencies:

```bash
```

```
npm install express mongoose body-parser ejs
```

3. Setting Up the Server with Express

Create a file called **server.js** to configure your Express server.

server.js:

```javascript
```

```javascript
const express = require('express');
const mongoose = require('mongoose');
const bodyParser = require('body-parser');
const path = require('path');
const app = express();

// Connect to MongoDB
mongoose.connect('mongodb://localhost:27017/blogApp', {
    useNewUrlParser: true,
    useUnifiedTopology: true
})
```

```
        .then(()    =>    console.log('Connected    to
MongoDB'))
    .catch(err => console.error(err));

// Middleware to parse incoming JSON data
app.use(bodyParser.urlencoded({  extended:  true
}));

// Set view engine
app.set('view engine', 'ejs');
app.set('views', path.join(__dirname, 'views'));

// Define routes
app.get('/', (req, res) => {
    res.render('index');  // Render the home page
});

// Start the server
app.listen(3000, () => {
    console.log('Server    is    running    on
http://localhost:3000');
});
```

In the code above:

- We connect to MongoDB using **Mongoose**.
- We use **EJS** as the view engine to render HTML files.
- **Body-parser** is used to parse incoming data from form submissions.

4. Defining Models for Blog Posts

Next, we define a **BlogPost** model using **Mongoose**. This model represents the data structure for a blog post.

Create a new directory called **models** and add a file called **blogPost.js**.

models/blogPost.js:

```javascript
const mongoose = require('mongoose');

// Create a schema for blog posts
const blogPostSchema = new mongoose.Schema({
    title: {
        type: String,
        required: true
    },
    content: {
        type: String,
        required: true
    },
    date: {
        type: Date,
        default: Date.now
    }
});
```

317

```
// Create a model from the schema
const    BlogPost    =    mongoose.model('BlogPost',
blogPostSchema);
```

```
module.exports = BlogPost;
```

5. Creating Routes for CRUD Operations

Let's add routes for **creating**, **reading**, **updating**, and **deleting** blog posts.

server.js (continued):

```
javascript
```

```
const BlogPost = require('./models/blogPost');
```

```
// Route to display all blog posts
app.get('/posts', async (req, res) => {
    const posts = await BlogPost.find();    //
Fetch all posts
    res.render('posts', { posts });
});
```

```
// Route to show form to create a new blog post
app.get('/new', (req, res) => {
    res.render('new');
});
```

```
// Route to handle new blog post creation
app.post('/posts', async (req, res) => {
    const { title, content } = req.body;
    const newPost = new BlogPost({ title, content
});
    await newPost.save();
    res.redirect('/posts');
});


// Route to delete a blog post
app.post('/delete/:id', async (req, res) => {
    await
BlogPost.findByIdAndDelete(req.params.id);
    res.redirect('/posts');
});
```

6. Creating Views for Displaying Posts

Now, let's create the **views** using **EJS** templates.

1. **views/index.ejs** (Home Page):

   ```
   html
   ```

   ```
   <h1>Welcome to the Blog</h1>
   <a href="/posts">View Blog Posts</a> | <a
   href="/new">Create New Post</a>
   ```

2. **views/posts.ejs** (List of Posts):

   ```
   html
   ```

319

```
<h1>Blog Posts</h1>
<ul>
    <% posts.forEach(post => { %>
        <li>
            <h2><%= post.title %></h2>
            <p><%= post.content %></p>
            <form        action="/delete/<%=
post._id %>" method="POST">
                <button
type="submit">Delete</button>
            </form>
        </li>
    <% }) %>
</ul>
<a href="/new">Create New Post</a>
```

3. **views/new.ejs** (Create New Post):

```
html
```

```
<h1>Create a New Blog Post</h1>
<form action="/posts" method="POST">
    <label for="title">Title:</label>
    <input     type="text"     name="title"
required>
    <label for="content">Content:</label>
    <textarea             name="content"
required></textarea>
```

320

```
<button                     type="submit">Create
Post</button>
</form>
```

Step 7: Running the Application

Run the application:

```
bash
```

```
node server.js
```

Visit `http://localhost:3000/` in your browser. You should be able to:

- View the list of blog posts.
- Create a new blog post.
- Delete existing blog posts.

Real-world Example: Building a Simple Blogging Platform

In this example, we've built a **blogging platform** using **Node.js**, **Express**, and **MongoDB**. The application allows users to:

- Create, view, and delete blog posts.
- Use **MongoDB** to store blog post data.
- Use **EJS** templates to render dynamic content on the front-end.

321

Summary

In this chapter, you:

- **Learned about full-stack JavaScript development**, where you use **Node.js**, **Express**, and **MongoDB** to build both the back-end and front-end of a web application.
- **Built a simple blogging platform** with **CRUD (Create, Read, Update, Delete)** functionality for managing blog posts.
- Gained hands-on experience with **Mongoose** for MongoDB interaction and **Express** for building RESTful routes.

By leveraging **JavaScript** for both the front-end and back-end, you can create powerful full-stack applications that are easier to manage and maintain. This chapter provides a solid foundation for building more complex full-stack applications.

www.ingramcontent.com/pod-product-compliance
Lightning Source LLC
LaVergne TN
LVHW051431050326
832903LV00030BD/3027